Safari for the Soul

Interior design and layout by Emily Coats
Cover design by Jason Olsen (www.jolsenmultimedia.com)

Publisher: Inkwater Press | www.inkwaterpress.com

Publisher's Cataloging-in-Publication
    Boal, Jan, author.
    Safari for the soul / by Jan Boal.
    pages cm
    Includes bibliographical references.
    LCCN 2015917298
    ISBN 978-1-62901-306-0 (pbk.)
    ISBN 978-1-62901-307-7 (Kindle)
    ISBN 978-1-62901-308-4 (ePub)

    1. Boal, Jan. 2. Animal rights activists--United States--Biography. 3. Psychiatric nurses--United States --Biography. 4. Safaris. 5. Endangered species. 6. Spiritual life. 7. Autobiographies. 8. Travel writing. I. Title.

    HV4716.B63A3 2016   179'.3092
                        QBI16-600004

Scan this QR Code to learn more about this title

Paperback
ISBN-13 978-1-62901-306-0 | ISBN-10 1-62901-306-4

Kindle
ISBN-13 978-1-62901-307-7 | ISBN-10 1-62901-307-2

ePub
ISBN-13 978-1-62901-308-4 | ISBN-10 1-62901-308-0

Printed in the U.S.A.

1   3   5   7   9   10   8   6   4   2

Safari for the SOUL

Ian Boal

PORTLAND•OREGON
INKWATERPRESS.COM

To my children Jennifer and Scott,

Never let fear stop you from creating your dreams.

Praise for *Safari for the Soul*

In a world where fear and self-doubt are routinely exploited for commercial and political gain, Jan challenged herself to open to a larger awareness.

Safari for the Soul, Ms. Boal's odyssey through Brazil, Greece, and Africa, became a personal odyssey of embracing her instincts and discovering true inner strength.

She offers a physical and emotional roadmap that promotes self-trust and sanity in the maelstrom that surrounds us.

CHAD MITCHELL, *The Chad Mitchell Trio*
Political Activist

Good read! Combining the spiritual with nature and animals, Jan's personal quest paves the way for readers to walk alongside her on a unique and thought provoking journey.

GARY LIVINGSTON, PhD
Chair, Providence Health Care Board of Directors, Spokane;
Chancellor, Spokane Community Colleges; and Superintendent,
Spokane School District, No. 81, Emeritus

CONTENTS

Acknowledgements

Of course without my mother none of this incredible quest or my writing *Safari for the Soul* would have been possible on so many levels. Mom, thank you for teaching me by example of what is inner strength and for your love and support.

My profound appreciation to my family and children who supported my wild adventurous spirit, venturing on my quest and then with writing *Safari for the Soul*. I love you all very much.

To my writing coach Julie, thank you for your knowledge and guidance. You were the first person placed on my path as soon as I said "okay Universe let's do it though I do not know what I am doing!"

For my editor, Lorna, THANK YOU!! No surprise you came on my path and how splendidly we connected, you so get me!

Jason, my artistic designer and media guru, dude, you are so awesome! What a great ride working together and becoming friends. It was no small coincidence, underscored with significant signs that we would partner up on this project.

Thank you all who helped me with the reading of my manuscript providing suggestions, encouragement and reviews. One after another so many wonderful people came into my life just at the right time, each time reassuring me faith in the Universe's plans that I was on the right track.

My gratitude to the Earthwatch organization, whose expeditions made my quest so fulfilling and fascinating. Thank you Drs, Silveira, Jacoma, Wahungu and Joan Gonzalvo. I feel privileged and proud to have worked alongside with each of you, your teams on these expeditions and all my fellow volunteers. What wonderful people you all are! It gives me inspiration and hope that we can save this planet on all planes that ails it and regain balance back in nature.

Inkwater staff, you are a class act! Sean, John, Emily and all the other behind the scenes crew, thank you for your support, patience and professionalism. It has been a pleasure.

Katie your funny wise ass wisdom and spiritual counsel always steered me right. A thousand hugs and blessings sending your way!

To Kathleen, your amazing friendship, kindness, listening ear and sense of direction, pushing me toward the right road, have meant the world to me. Thank you very much.

I have been blessed with the friendships I developed with my co-workers at Kootenai Medical Center who inspired me with their dedication and professionalism with working with the mentally ill. Thank you for your inputs and support while I was undergoing my writing of *Safari for the Soul*. A special thank you my dear Kerstin for your endearing friendship.

Thank you, thank you, thank you from the bottom of my heart for all the love and continuous support over the years from my dear Ya Yas: Yvette, Becky, Rosalie, Michelle, Deb, Susie, Sharon, Lori and Cola. You rock my world!

A special note of gratitude for my side kicks, my dog, Buddy and cat, Captain Jack, who were always by my side unconditionally and lovingly.

And thank you John, for your love and choosing to walk beside me on this new path.

Preface

I became a psychiatric nurse at 40. The age at which this happened may be a bit surprising, but the fact that I wanted to help others was always pretty obvious. Sometimes it just takes us a bit longer to recognize our calling.

Mine happens to be standing up for those who cannot protect themselves, whether because they have no voice to speak or because the voices they hear are feeding them bad information. Even when those with mental illnesses do find the strength to speak, they are almost universally ignored. At one time, each of these people was someone's brand-new baby, with all the potential and expectations that entails. Then, their brains got sick, or the people around them contaminated their innocence, or a host of other things may have happened; and suddenly—they are unseen.

In my profession, I especially enjoy the role of patient advocate. It is important for patients to know that they are seen and heard. Even if I am certain that the patient in front of me isn't actually confronted by the devil every night when she gets up to pee, she needs to be heard. The sophistication and severity of patients' delusions can be fascinating, but what is ever so much more intriguing is how strong the instinct to survive becomes. Every day, they survive through hallucinations, through depression, through addictions and self-doubt.

My choice is to see and hear these patients; to support them and work with them to find treatments and therapies that can lessen the difficulties they face. If those treatments and therapies don't have the desired effect, we keep searching—together. I've had patients who needed only small doses of medication to manage depression, while others have only found relief through electroconvulsive therapy. I've also seen the power of laughter, music, and movement as tools that can be just as effective as psychiatric medications.

And, it's all beautiful. It's all important. It is my calling.

When we live a life that is true to our own beliefs and desires, we find our calling. In answering that call and following where it leads, we can maximize our own potential and contribute so much to the planet, as well as all those who dwell upon it. Of course, this isn't always easy. When there is so much to be done on a daily basis, there's no time to listen for a call and no energy to change directions. Inertia keeps us going, with our eyes down and our ears full of new car ads and cereal jingles. The outside voices continually tell us what we *should* want, and they make sure they do it loud enough to drown out the voice that tells us what we *truly* want.

People call this voice a lot of different things: God, Dharma, Great Spirit...I call it the Universe. When you are true to yourself, you are true to this voice. When you take care of yourself, you are creating energy that is positive and benefits not only yourself, but those around you, your community, even the planet we all share.

I was fortunate to be in a place where I was able to hear the voice and to respond to it. My hope is to empower you to do the same. Perhaps your voice isn't telling you to go to Africa (or maybe it is!), but chances are that if you listen, you will discover that it has amazing things in store for you. The challenge is to answer your calling. Your story will be different from mine, but when you let go of fear, trust your intuition, and nurture your spirit, it will be no less spectacular.

CHAPTER 1

Lake Roosevelt, Washington

"**Y**ou could travel the world, Jan."

While the idea itself seemed a little out of left field, the even more puzzling mystery of the moment was where the heck that voice was coming from. I was alone in my car, on my way to work in the cold winter weather that had laid unabashed claim to the Pacific Northwest. It was December, and I had been using the day's commute to reflect on the things one normally does as the year draws to a close. What lessons had 2010 taught me? What did I want the New Year to bring?

The preceding year had been marked by loss and filled with grief. I was contemplating building my retirement home on Lake Roosevelt, Washington, and though it should have been a joyous time in my life, it was marred by the fact that this was no longer going to be "our" retirement home. After 27 years of marriage, I had recently divorced. I didn't regret the choice to divorce, just as I didn't regret the marriage. Sure, there had been some not-so-good times, but there were wonderful ones, as well. All of them together had certainly provided me plenty of growth opportunities and helped me to become the woman I was at that moment. And yet, I was grieving the loss of the relationship, the loss of the love, and the loss of the familiar.

The year had also brought death and confusion. My step-father Morey passed away at the beginning of the year, and in addition to mourning his death, I was forced to watch as my grief-stricken, 73-year-old mother maneuvered through her own sorrow. They, too, were together for more than 27 years, and were the absolute loves of each others' lives. She had been so happy with him, and Morey adored her.

And so, I found myself behind the wheel of my car, determining how to shed the pain of the previous year. I was actually looking forward to building the house on the lake. In my mind, it would become a happy gathering place for family and friends. In addition to being a home, it would also serve as a retreat where I would lead the workshops I had developed to help guide other women out of patterns of living in fear. The workshop had already been successful, empowering women to face and understand their fears, as well as the negative self-talk that has been conditioned into so many of us by the sometimes suffocating beliefs thrust upon us by family, culture, and society.

My hope was to expand the Finding Your Heaven on Earth workshop into a full retreat. It would provide a safe, nurturing place where women could learn how to be at peace with themselves, even when it felt like they were surrounded by complete chaos. My motivation wasn't completely altruistic, of course, as part of the drive to develop the retreat was to show my mom and myself that we would be OK, too. Both our lives had unexpectedly changed, and it felt like an opportunity to redefine ourselves. Personally, I was ready to move onward, even if I had to take baby steps to do so. I needed something to look forward to, something to build and create, a new way to experience myself and the world around me.

That's when the voice chimed in: "You could travel the world, Jan." I looked around the empty car to pinpoint the source of the statement. No one was there, so it would appear that the voice had come from somewhere within me. I sighed and smiled. Even those who don't believe in astrology often find that their zodiac sign fits them uncannily well. I was a Gemini, the twins, and I had come to refer to the "other" voice in my head as my counterpart, Gem. The two of us together were Gem 'n' I.

This time around, though, I didn't think Gem had much of an argument. I had done plenty of traveling already. It was time for me to settle down and get grounded. Why, in July I went to Kauai, Hawaii for the first time and learned how to surf. I had dreamed of riding the waves since I was a teenager and took advantage of my family's partial ownership of a condo on the north side of the island to make it come true. I had felt a little out of place, sure. I mean, who ever heard of a middle-aged woman up and deciding to surf? But I found myself flourishing among the brilliant colors of the hibiscus and the intoxicating scent of plumeria.

Of course, I was probably more like the bird of paradise flower: lots of color and character, a bit spiky and weird, but still beautiful in my own way as I took to the turquoise water with determination. During my stay, I met while surfing, a famous (and very handsome) actor who had a vacation home on the island. "See, I was meant to be a surfer!" I told myself, as this was obviously a sign from the Universe that I was where I was supposed to be. Speaking of handsome, the male surfers of all ages certainly lent a little something extra to the trip. Whether it was the lush green mountains or the beautiful toned bodies of the men, there was a lovely sight to behold no matter where my eyes fell.

Only a mere four months after that excursion, my daughter and I had flown to England together for a family event. We met up with my mom, brother, and aunt to join the 50th anniversary celebration of an uncle and his wife. This was my first trip overseas since the ripe old age of 21, and we took advantage of the opportunity to travel through the countryside. There was tea with scones, stone cottages, gray skies, and all the other things necessary for a true English experience.

So, *clearly*, I had traveled. I was good. Gem didn't know what she was talking about.

The idea wouldn't be dismissed that easily, however. The rest of the drive found me lost in thought, imagining myself off in some far-flung land getting to know the culture directly from the locals who lived it on a daily basis. Instead of turning to the nightly news for a biased view of world events, perhaps I could learn to understand them first-hand. Ah, but with cultural misunderstandings and political strife, it didn't make sense for me to put myself in harm's way. I was a single woman, and traveling the world alone was not safe. Right? There's terrorism, and bandits, and war lords. There are con men and thieves and any other number of things to fear. My heart and thoughts were racing, but it wasn't because I was scared. I tried to be rational, to talk myself down, but I couldn't shake the image of me walking the streets in a foreign country, maybe shopping at a market using newly-acquired language skills or perhaps even being invited to a local's home for a meal. What about my job? My kids? While the original intention of invoking my children was to convince myself I was crazy, the argument backfired on me when I realized that this point in all of our lives actually provided a unique window of opportunity for something like this to happen. My two kids were young adults who had become independent and were defining their own lives separate from mine. No one was on the verge of marriage or expecting a child, events that I would not have missed "for the world," so to speak.

For my part, I wasn't currently involved in a serious romantic relationship, so I wouldn't have to consider a partner's feelings. My job, on the other hand, was unlikely to offer me a leave of absence. If I wanted to be gone for more than a month, I would have to quit, knowing that would mean leaving a secure position, not to mention job hunting again upon my return. This was definitely something to take into consideration, and yet it didn't entirely dampen my enthusiasm. The excitement and uncertainty swirled in my stomach. I didn't want to be too rash about anything, but I was wasn't willing to close the door on the idea altogether, either.

As I turned in to the parking lot at work, I put the final touches on my plan for the day. I would run the idea by some of my friends and co-workers to gauge whether I had lost my marbles or if this really was feasible. I would also keep an eye out for signs that seemed to encourage or discourage this runaway train of thought. Hey, it worked in Kauai, why not at the office?

Since it was the week before Christmas, some of the folks at work were doing a Secret Santa gift exchange. My Secret Santa had apparently been a busy little elf; when I arrived in my office, there was a small present on the desk, wrapped and waiting for me to notice it. I happen to love surprises and was smiling as I removed the bright paper from the flat, rectangular package. It was a calendar for the upcoming year. My mouth may have actually fallen open when I noticed that the title was "Passport to the World." The calendar was a collection of photos from around the world.

I had asked for a sign, but I didn't expect it seconds after walking through the door! I shared what had happened in the car with my coworkers and showed them the calendar. I hadn't been sure what to expect when I told people about my hair-brained idea. Would they encourage me to *carpe diem*? Would they point out the safety concerns? Would they just roll their eyes and say, "There she goes again!" It turns out that I needn't have worried, as everyone was completely supportive.

In fact, they expressed that I was exactly the type of person who could pull off something like this, which is certainly what I needed to hear. "You have great people skills, Jan," one coworker said. "You're friendly and outgoing and would be great at meeting new people!" "You're street smart," another added. At the time, I was working as an outpatient psychiatric nurse, a job that definitely hones one's street smarts. Bolstered by their words and enthusiasm, I started to seriously consider embarking on a quest.

It's not surprising that I immediately started thinking of my trip in terms of a "quest." The spiritual leanings of my adult life have tended to be rather eclectic, with a fair amount of my beliefs influenced by Native American teachings. Growing up, my brothers and I were raised with a salad bar approach to religious education. Our parents encouraged us to sample different things to find out what worked for each of us individually. We didn't attend church together, although we did occasionally go along with friends when invited. This meant that we got a smattering of different traditions and were able to see how other people integrated them into their own lives.

My mother had an interest in alternative spiritual beliefs that were definitely outside the mainstream at that time. She studied astrology and taught classes for others wanting to learn how to formulate astrological charts. Psychics were regularly invited into our home to do readings, and my older brother eventually went on to marry a woman who performed tarot card readings. These things weren't presented to us as anything other than additional means to connect with ourselves and the world around us. As a result, I grew up comfortable with a pretty wide variety of people and beliefs, and I have often felt that a reading, chart, or tarot spread is dead-on accurate for me.

For a number of years leading up to that morning in the car, I had been enamored with the idea of doing a vision quest. I was drawn to and intrigued by many spiritual traditions of the Native American culture. Through my readings on these topics, I learned that many of the practices are routes to looking inward and reflecting in order to achieve personal growth. These experiences are enhanced as one learns to trust the Great Spirit—God, the Universe—enough to recognize signs and guidance as they appear along one's personal path.

A vision quest is one of the many ways to welcome the knowledge that comes along with this way of thinking. It can be used as a means to connect with a person's authentic self, as well as the earth. Many times, a vision quest entails a journey into nature that provides the opportunity for introspection as a person examines and answers personal questions that rise from within. A vision quest doesn't necessarily have to be that formal, however. Sometimes it involves nothing more than a day of solitude in a specially prepared room that promotes peace and thoughtfulness.

I had already begun to ask and answer some of those internal questions for myself, but I had been yearning for a way to go further. With such a variety of influences, I had found a form of spirituality that worked well for me. I made a point to ask the Universe for daily guidance and tried to pay attention to what might be holding sway over me at any given time—was it the energy of myself or others, or maybe the subliminal effects of my environment? I often felt as if my intuition was trying to guide me, even going so far as to give me visions about the course my life would or could take. In fact, when thoughts would arise out of nowhere, I considered them to be the voices of my spiritual guides, offering me the answers I sought, as long as I was willing to accept them.

And, there were always the coincidences. I had reached the point where it often felt that coincidences were anything but. Instead, if I could only interpret them, I would see they were signs clearly pointing me in the right direction. For example, the first day I decided to separate from my husband, I shared the news with my hairdresser of five years. Unbeknownst to me, she had just left her husband and had found an agency that rented out the homes of snow-birds—people who spend their summers in the North and their winters in the South. She allowed me to stay with her for a month, and then I was able to sublet a beautiful home near work from the same agency. To me, this seemed like such a positive sign that I was being looked after.

Those not-so-coincidental coincidences often happened when job-hunting. I would find a job that I was sure was a perfect fit, so much so that I would practically be choosing my first-day-of-work outfit while I was still in the interview. I would be crushed when the job fell through, but without fail, something much better—a better fit, a better paycheck—would arise out of seemingly nowhere. It started to look to me like I was supposed to succeed. They let me know when I was on the right track, too. That force—my spirit guides, guardian angels, whatever it is that looks out for me—has proven especially adept at giving me signs through the material I happen to be reading. I'll be enjoying a book unsuspectingly when all of a sudden a passage will jump out that offers information or support a decision I've been contemplating.

I felt as if a vision quest would provide me the chance

to delve deeper into these ideas and to uncover whether or not there was any substance to them. I am a very open and accepting person, but I also like to have things proven to me rather than always be expected to take things at face value. If I were to follow through, to actually take the first step on such a quest, it wouldn't just be about having an exotic vacation. It would be more of a test. I would test the Universe to see if it really was offering me all that I thought it was. I would test myself to find what kind of strength I actually possessed. I would seek signs and consciously attempt to interpret and follow them to further develop my own spirituality. It did not escape my attention, either, that such a quest would also be about really opening myself up to grow and change. It would be a broadening.

The choice to embark on this particular quest only took a couple of days. Seeing the signs and feeling in my heart that I was ready, I set out to craft an adventure for myself. In hopes of saving some money, I determined that I would do my own research and make my own travel arrangements. The effort required was fairly extensive, but when I look back now, I see that in doing so, I allowed myself considerable freedom to accept and work with the surprises that would arise throughout the journey.

The biggest initial challenge was to sift through the deluge of ideas and options that flooded my mind. The whole world was my oyster, and I had to determine which pearls to pluck. An arctic trek? An insider's view of Tokyo? Perhaps I should do a silent retreat with the monks in Tibet?

The Internet offered a dizzying array of choices. I finally had to take a deep breath and remind myself that this was about trusting the Universe. How could I expect it show me what I needed to do if I was dead-set on controlling it? I maintained my excitement but trusted that things would work out as they should.

Instead of simply throwing darts at a map, though, I considered what my priorities were. The fact that I was blessed with both the means and the time for such a bold undertaking left me certain that somehow giving back to the planet should be a high priority. In each country I chose to visit, I would volunteer to do research on endangered animals. I would be a part of something positive, something I believed in. It was almost like a two-for-one deal. I could learn about different cultures from an anthropological perspective, but I could also educate myself more fully on the experience of animals that I had so far only learned of through documentaries and books.

This idea also sat well with me because I saw that starting each leg of my quest with an established endangered species protection group would provide a safe place in which to get acclimated and comfortable. My safety was certainly at the top of my list of concerns, as I knew I would likely be traveling in countries where women were considered second-class and/or a target for harassment or violence. In some places, kidnappings and robberies are common if one doesn't take measured precautions. On top of that, Americans aren't always the most favored of tourists, another factor to consider during the planning process.

Years earlier, an organization called Earthwatch had sponsored a high school science competition that earned my daughter and 99 other students a scientific research trip with one of their groups. Their work focuses on conservation research, and they offer volunteers a chance to join in field research all over the world. Volunteers pay—donate really—anywhere from $1,500 to $5,000 to become part of the expedition. The cost depends upon location and the number of days the volunteer wishes to participate. It's an ingenious method of fundraising, as the money goes to support the cost of research and the salaries of Earthwatch staff members, as well as food and lodging for the volunteers.

By working with the organization, I felt better able to address some of my safety concerns. I would set up an itinerary to be with Earthwatch at the beginning of each leg, and in addition to staying with them, I also had access to their safe and affordable hotel listings for when I traveled alone after the expeditions. Earthwatch envisions a world where we all live within our means, benefitting nature, rather than always taking from her what we want. To that end, I would be staying in many eco-friendly camps and rubbing elbows with others who shared this dream.

I had one other ace in the hole when it came to safety. As a psychiatric nurse, I was well-trained in what is called MOAB, or Management of Aggressive Behavior. This training teaches self-defense and other safe techniques for managing patients with aggressive, violent, or unsafe behaviors. I felt fairly confident in my training and wouldn't think twice about head-butting someone or taking them to the ground if I needed to. My history of working in an outpatient outreach program with the mentally ill had put me in some fairly precarious places to assist patients: back alleys, rough neighborhoods, inside drug houses. I was good at assessing my surroundings, knowing where the exits were, and not keeping my back to anyone.

There were also smart travel precautions I would combine with my training. It was imperative not to let my guard down when I was alone, not to take valuables with me, and to split up my money when I carried it, so if some was stolen, it wasn't *all* stolen. I've always been friendly, and my ability to meet new people and set them at ease would be an asset. I would check in with the staff at the hotels and hostels to let them know of my comings and goings and would engage locals to ask questions. Sure, most of these things wouldn't come in all that handy if I met a lion or something, but they would be pretty helpful in keeping me safe from people with ill intentions.

I was already picturing myself hanging out with famous scientists while tracking rare species all over the world. I would be cool, but serious, while working diligently to protect the hunted and make a small difference in the planet's favor. I imagined myself in Tanzania, as though in a National Geographic episode. There I would be, sitting in a jeep with my safari hat, watching rapt as the wildebeest migrated across the plains. I hadn't even left, but my imagination was already on safari.

My favorite animal was the jaguar. In fact, I had come to think of the beautiful cats as my own totem. Certainly a quest like the one I was designing should bring me to the jaguar. I knew that Earthwatch had an expedition tracking jaguars, and suddenly I was booked for a five-week stay in Brazil. This was an accomplishment to be savored. I had yet to set foot on a plane or pack a single item into my suitcase, and yet booking that trip to Brazil made the entire experience real for the first time. I began to comprehend that I would soon be in the heart of the world's largest wet eco-system, hearing the call of the birds and meeting people who worked hands-on with my beloved jaguar.

Whether it was my preoccupation with jaguars or the Universe itself validating my decision, I found the sleek cat making its way into my dreams. Twice it came to me, saying, "Find me," and "I know your medicine." I was more than willing to accept the offer, and I became convinced that I was going to have my very own jaguar encounter in Brazil. I didn't allow myself to focus on the how or why of it; rather, I relinquished control and waited for the magic to happen.

Ideas for my quest were coming fast and furious. I tried to map out all of my places of interest, quickly discovering that it included pretty much the whole world: the Virgin Islands, Australia, New Zealand, Egypt, Ethiopia, Mexico, parts of Asia. I investigated what Earthwatch expeditions were available in these areas and when. The African continent called to me, but the excitement I felt over the prospect was tempered by a significant nervous energy. There was a lot of political unrest in parts of Africa, and a single woman traveling alone could find herself in some compromising situations, to say the least.

I had heard that South Africa was particularly beautiful and a must-see location, but for some reason, my heart strings kept pulling me toward Uganda. There was an expedition in a remote area that afforded an opportunity to view the amazingly rare silverback gorilla. It is quite likely that the mountain gorilla will become extinct in my children's lifetime, and I felt compelled to be a witness to their existence, to act as the eyes of future grandchildren who might be denied the privilege.

As I debated where my quest would take me, an unexpected opportunity arose. A friend invited me to join her, her husband, and some friends in Puerto Vallarta in June. I had looked into visiting some of Mexico's ruins several years before, and I still had June available on my schedule. I could spend May in Brazil, come home for a couple of days in June, and then head off to Mexico. I found it amusing that such a random invitation would prompt me to purchase the first actual airline ticket for my adventure.

With May and June now planned, it occurred to me that I didn't really know how long my quest was going to be. I felt like it had to be at least three months long to really get the experience I was looking for. I needed to give the Universe and myself both time if I was going to test us like this. I wasn't sure that I wanted to be away from home for an entire year, though, as that seemed like it could be exhausting and possibly counter-productive. I decided to leave things open-ended and go wherever the wind happened to blow me.

Since I was going to be flying over the Virgin Islands on my way to Brazil, logic told me that it would be rude not to stop for a visit. I may have been making up excuses, but I really wanted to go to the Virgin Islands! I added it to my itinerary and decided to get creative with lodging by checking out a database called Couchsurfing. People all over the world offer their homes, a room, or even a literal couch that travelers can use for free or cheap. I mulled the idea over, not wanting to find myself like that lady who went to the Bate's Motel in *Psycho*. The appeal, though, was pretty strong, since I knew it would give me the opportunity to meet locals and experience real life on the Islands instead of staying in a commercial environment. I wanted to embrace the cultures of the places I visited. I made plans to stay in a small studio apartment for $20 a day on St. Thomas and then to stay with a single woman my age on St. John.

I want to say that it's too bad that many of my initial plans fell through, but I'm not actually disappointed. While I did end up enjoying the hospitality of that lovely lady in the Virgin Islands, the trip to Mexico was not to be. The Universe had other plans. It prodded me along, opened up all the right doors, and got my schedule cleared for the month of June because it had something else in store for me entirely. Of course, I didn't know that yet, so I still had my sights set on bikinis and tequilla-based drinks at that point. I had no idea that instead of margaritas and mariachis, I would find myself wearing layers of protective clothing and sifting through someone else's memories.

Researching what countries to visit, what to see, and where to stay was time consuming, but it was also very exciting and educational. I would develop lists of places to consider, then cross-reference them with Earthwatch expeditions, then cross-reference *those* cross-references with seasonal data—taking into consideration the seasonal differences of the Northern and Southern hemispheres, then determine what other activities I might want to engage in on my own after the expedition. In some cases, I would arrange all my lodging and transportation in advance, although the people I met through Earthwatch would help with some of that when I got there.

Putting the trip together also required me to do some pretty serious studying of the cultures I would be visiting. Even simple greetings differ drastically from one place to another. I needed to know whether I should be shaking hands, kissing cheeks, or bowing without making eye contact! Things would be even dicier considering the wide variety of languages I expected to encounter. Was I going to be able to get by on English? Maybe I should take a pocket dictionary. Exchanging money was another concern. I made sure, too, that I had the number to the American Embassy in each and every country I was going to visit. I also bought all kinds of travel books, such as *Lonely Planet* and *National Audubon*, that provided ideas on places to visit, restaurants, prices for accommodations, and more.

I did a lot of this research online, but I also reached out to interview people who had been to the places I was considering. My friend Don reassured me, saying, "Jannie, you will love Africa. It is very spiritual and you will learn about getting in touch with yourself." He suggested that I travel to Mozambique, Zanzibar, and Mombasa. He'd lived in Kenya for two and a half years with the Peace Corps in a small village that didn't even have fresh water when he first arrived. His job had been to help the tribe learn trading skills, and he was instrumental in building their clean water system. Don even hooked me up with a friend of his from the village who had become a marathon runner for Kenya. I was going to get my own personal tour in Nairobi! He also gave me practical advice, such as, "Jannie, you have to haggle with the taxi drivers or they won't respect you." Other well-traveled friends and peers offered me all kinds of advice, stories of their good (and bad) experiences traveling, and hints and tips for saving money.

Gem 'n' I had plenty to discuss. The dual aspect of my nature led me to a whole lot of mind changing. It wasn't unusual for me to go back and forth on decisions, but that tendency was pretty magnified when there were literally thousands of miles between two choices. Rather than getting too bogged down in the minutia of every leg of the journey, I chose instead to use the expedition sites as a sort of home base of operations. I would have a couple of ideas of what I wanted to do after the expeditions were over, but I would keep my schedule fairly well open to allow for adventures to present themselves. I would follow the signs on a whim and be more apt to stay in the moment instead of trying to stick to an agenda.

Keeping a flexible schedule doesn't mean that I didn't have plenty of details to attend to, though. Fortunately, my passport was up-to-date after last year's trip to Great Britain. Visas, however, were a bit trickier. Some countries required me to have the visa in advance in order to enter, while others had them available to purchase on arrival. Because of this, I had to coordinate the purchase of each overseas airline tickets to coincide with the specific dates, lengths of stay, and accommodations in mind. It felt like a bit of a hassle to jump through so many hoops, but it paid off. Since I took care of so much of it online, I found the occasional well-placed door opening for me, such as the time I happened to land on a wholesale international flight web site that saved me half the price on my fare to Greece and then on to Africa. Half price tickets? Yes, please!

Itinerary planning was going beautifully until I hit a glitch. I had found an incredible price for air fare between Greece and Africa, but my credit card was declined. I started to get frantic because the price was set to go up in the next day or two, and I also had to get my visa application in based on the flight arrangements. It was getting down to the wire for everything to be processed and back to me before the departure date, but my card kept being blocked. Everything had gone so well up to this point, and I couldn't wrap my head around what the problem might be since there were no other charges on that card.

"OK, Jan. Remain calm," I told myself. I'm sure the picture of me at that moment did not reflect the advice I was giving myself. My pulse was racing, and I had been on the computer since early that morning trying to finalize my itinerary. It was now mid-afternoon, I was still in my sweats without having bathed, and my curly hair resembled a side of Spaghetti-Os that had taken a couple of spins in the blender. Trying not to lose it, I emailed the online agent. As I sent my electronic SOS, I had one of those ah-ha moments and knew clearly that something was about to change regarding Africa.

My intuition told me that the purchase had been blocked for a reason, and I chose to accept it. The next day I received a phone call from Earthwatch letting me know there had been a mix-up. I had planned on joining the Samburu Tribe expedition in Kenya, but that particular session was only for teens. Unless I was an adult chaperone for the trip, I would not be allowed to join. "Teenagers?!" I thought. "Yeah...no. I'm good. I'll go ahead and pass on this one."

Still, I was disappointed. I had wanted to work with the Samburu tribe on biodiversity with the endangered Grevy's zebra. Since I was going to study jaguars in Brazil and dolphins in Greece, I thought working with a tribe would add some great variety. Plus, I wanted some first-hand cultural experience. I had studied dance in high school and college, and it had long been my dream to witness a tribal dance of celebration. Since that expedition wouldn't work, I was told that there was a black rhino tour available during the same time frame, and I was welcome to be a part of it.

I agreed to the second expedition, knowing that it would be interesting, as well. I had an inkling just then that told me, "There must be a reason I'm going on the black rhino expedition. Too bad about not meeting that tribe, though." I had no idea how right—and wrong—that thought would be.

During the three months of preparations, I was adamant about spending time only with people who were positive and supportive of my quest. I made a point to steer clear of skepticism, negative people, and even negative thoughts in my own head. If you were going to be a wet blanket, I wasn't interested. We've all had nay-sayers in our lives, those who are reacting to your experiences out of their own fear; but this was not a time for me to accept that.

All I could do was laugh at the people who asked, "What if something happens?" That was precisely what I was banking on—something happening! I didn't know what that might be, but I was sure it was going to be awesome. I believed that I was being guided in the right direction and that only the best was in store for me. Throughout my life, I'd often been referred to as a "free spirit," but it wasn't until after my divorce that I figured out what this meant. Originally, I thought people were calling me spunky, and I had an idea that a free spirit was someone running through the fields with daisies in her hair and a far-away look in her eyes.

Instead, I realized that the adventurous soul residing within my petite frame was likely akin to the great explorers of the past. Our restlessness doesn't mean we are unhappy or even unsatisfied; rather, it's in our nature to seek out new things and to savor the experiences that ensue.

I recognized that those who were cautious or even pessimistic about my plans were often coming from a perspective of fear rather than a desire to repress the inquisitive and outgoing nature of my overactive imagination and lust for adventure. These fear-based behaviors are taught, they are passed down through generations as a part of the culture in which we live. Those who love us do not want to see us hurt, led astray, or suffer, so much so that they fear it. I am a parent, and therefore, I am as guilty as the next person. But I have also learned that we are all different and have varying needs that should be explored without shame or guilt. I wish I would have been better at that when I was raising my children.

As my quest drew closer, however, I began to trust myself more and to be less concerned with others' negative opinions. While the majority of my friends and family were wonderfully supportive, I was especially surprised by how enthusiastic total strangers were. Women, especially, would say things like, "You go, girl. You do this for the rest of us women who can't!" I simply knew it was the right path for me, and the way everything flowed so easily went on to confirm it.

April 15th was my last day at work. A mish-mash of feelings competed for my attention. On the one hand, I was about to embark on what would certainly be the adventure of a lifetime. I was ready to heed the call and could not have been more exhilarated about it. On the other hand, it was coming at the cost of the best job I had ever had. Not only was I leaving a place I loved, but when I returned from this adventure, I would have to start all over somewhere else, with no guarantee that I would be anywhere near as happy. As a nurse, I felt confident in my ability to gain employment when I went looking for it; and if worse came to worse, I could probably work part time and enjoy semi-retirement.

The following day there was a bon voyage party at my house. The place was packed from wall to wall, with folks spilling out into the garage to dance to the live band. I was surrounded by friends and family, all of whom offered words of love and affirmation. The air was electric with positive energy, and the smiles and laughter were contagious. My dear friend Yvette even decorated a cake with little plastic animals and a safari helmet. We had spent plenty of time during the last few months joking about how I would drive the flight attendants crazy with constant pestering of "Are we there yet? Are we? Are we? How about now?"

The party itself was a testament to real friendship. There is a particular group of about ten of us who call ourselves the Ya-Yas. The ladies surprised me with a poem and presented me with a small ceramic swan that fit in my palm. A few years before, we had all gotten together for a girls' weekend at a resort, and I got the idea of "borrowing" one of the decoy swans used to scare away geese. Sammy the Swan was unceremoniously bird-napped and she lived it up—drinking, dancing, and singing with the band. I dubbed my new travel partner "Little Sammy" and thanked my Ya-Yas, letting them know that she would be appearing in photos all over the world.

The last week before departure arrived, bringing with it no lack of details to attend to and loose ends that needed tying up. Amidst the bustle of packing, shopping, and taking care of arrangements for my house and belongings, I was also doing my best to spend as much time as possible with my family, and also with my friend Allen. We had a casual romantic relationship going, but it wasn't something that we felt was a long-term commitment. We had a similar goofy sense of humor and could talk for hours about spirituality and personal insights, but he was more of a stay-at-home fellow while I wanted to go off and conquer the world. So, we'd decided to see each other through the winter, knowing that when I climbed aboard that airplane, our farewell would be about more than me taking a trip. Our friendship would undoubtedly continue, but we would no longer be lovers.

I spent my last day with Allen out on the lake. We were comfortable with each other, but there was an underlying tension in the evening that made my skin prickle. After all the time we'd spent there at his cabin, going over the latest plans for my quest, it was bittersweet to come to this point. I was preparing to embark on my future, but with the knowledge that what we had would simply become "the past." My feelings were all jumbled together and left me feeling sentimental and nostalgic for what I would be leaving behind.

"It's between you and your maker now, and the road in front of you," Allen offered as we parted ways. We would stay in touch, and during my quest, he was always willing to offer sound advice or a shoulder to cry on from an ocean away.

CHAPTER 2

Brazil: The Araguaia Corridor

The jaguar—or panther—is smaller than lions or tigers, but it is fiercer. This cat can climb, run, and even swim better than its bulkier relatives. According to the Arawak people, everything has jaguar in it. They say that nothing can exist without it. The jaguar has more than 5,000 voluntary muscles in its body, just waiting for the animal to call upon them to slink, pounce, or stretch in the sun on a hot, lazy day.

The grace of this animal is inspiring. It can move with an effortless appearance or freeze entirely, even mid-stride. The jaguar is an excellent sprinter but is less adept at long distances. Still, they roam vast areas as they hunt for food and search for a mate.

The courtship between male and female is intense, but it does not last, and the female raises cubs on her own. When *they gain their independence at about a year, so does she, returning to her solitary life. The jaguar is able to bite through the temporal bones of an animal's skull, and they have been known to shear off the heads of their prey with a single swipe of their claws. This strength and independence has undoubtedly played into the long-held belief amongst cultures that the black panther is a symbol of the feminine, the dark mother. She represents the darkness, along with the death and rebirth which spring from it, all the while helping us to understand the power inherent in these sometimes disquieting aspects of existence. In acknowledging the associated fears, we are able to eliminate them and internalize the power they hold.*

Like all cats, the jaguar has binocular vision, allowing each eye to work singularly and providing a greater depth of vision. This allows her to magnify images and facilitates a remarkable ability to judge distances. It is said that those who—like me—align with the jaguar develop a greater depth of vision in their own lives, seeing deeply into events and other people, as well as themselves. More than a shift in perception, this becomes an "inner knowing."

Throughout my experiences in Brazil, I found that my own inner knowing continued to expand. I grew to listen to and trust it, as I was shown its accuracy again and again. I became certain that I would have a personal interaction with a jaguar. I could not fathom how, nor did I try to imagine it in order to remain present and without expectations when it happened. This openness provided the opportunity for the Universe to surprise me with many, many gifts. By letting go, I was able to let the Universe give these gifts to me, and they were so much more beautiful than anything I could have imagined on my own.

At the core of my quest—my adventure, my journey—were always the people I encountered. Through them, I was gifted a glimpse into the human experience and a deeper understanding of the role our cultural differences play in the way we perceive reality. Like me, many of them came from faraway lands to play a part in the preservation of the jaguar. From the friendly chit-chat of new acquaintances, to the deep philosophical conversations of those striving to truly grasp one another's views, to the physical communication that takes place between lovers, Brazil continually thrust me into new, intense relationships of all stripes. Knowing, and being known, by these beautiful people expanded my own reality. Both my mind and my view of the world opened like a blossom warmed by the early rays of the morning sun. Like that bloom, my soul would continue to open, soaking up all the light and warmth that the universe chose to shine upon me.

There were many reasons for the intensity of these relationships. The cultural unfamiliarity was a bonding experience for those of us who traveled long distances to be a part of the expedition. Our general proximity to one another as we lived and worked together fostered a strong sense of community. Of course, there was also the earnestness and passion we all felt to protect the animals. The evenings spent partaking of the caipirinha, the local alcoholic drink, probably didn't hurt either.

My arrival in the bustling city of Goiania was marked by what would become a familiar set of rituals centered around checking in and unloading luggage. With this accomplished, I set out in search of Caroline. Members of the expedition had received information about each other prior to our departures, and this Brit and I had taken the opportunity to exchange a few emails. Caroline was young and charismatic with a background working in various banking departments for 18 years. It was exciting to learn that she had quite a bit of travel experience, but the real thrill was knowing that she had participated in the Black Rhino expedition in Kenya. It was like the stars had aligned for me to meet someone who could share first-hand what I might expect from one of the expeditions on my agenda.

Unfortunately, Caroline was out and about, taking in the sights of what would be our new home. Rather than doing the same on my own, I chose to hang out at the hotel and relax—or, you know, try to keep from drowning in anticipation—before connecting with my group of soon-to-be scientific researchers. The team finally met in the foyer that afternoon. Caroline had been sightseeing with another team member named Greg. He was a business man and teacher from Australia; and of the four of us, he was the only one who had been to Brazil before. Greg had studied Portuguese for a number of years and visited as often as possible to submerge himself in both the language and the culture that he so loved. It felt like a little a victory to know we had a comrade who spoke the language.

Our fourth member was Barbara, also from Britain. It turned out that she and Caroline lived fairly close to one another back in their home country. That said, they had never met, and for someone from my background, it was extraordinary to hear how strikingly different their accents were. I was already enamored by the experience of our communication being seasoned with such a variety of international accents. While beautiful, I quickly learned that having to pay such close attention to others' words—constantly watching the shape of their mouths, or translating idioms across cultures—can actually be quite fatiguing. Thus began the use of a phrase that I would not be able to retire until my quest finally came to an end: "Sorry? What was that you said?"

Barbara was a striking woman in her 60s whose favorite companion was her blind beagle, Barney. She, too, enjoyed traveling, and by the end of that first night in Brazil, she had us in tears laughing as she recounted tales of her escapades as a tourist in Greece. Apparently she once drank too much ouzo and could not seem to avoid tripping on the same bush over and over, no matter how wide of a girth she tried to give it. The bush proved victorious in the end, with the Brit coming out of the kerfuffle looking like a beaten wrestler but laughing like a very good sport. Her willingness to share that story on our first night led us to nicknaming our new compatriot "Barbara Bush."

The next morning, we were on our way to the Araguaia. Travel would take 14 hours, mostly by bus. As the only one with knowledge of Portuguese, Greg spent two of those hours as my personal tutor, providing me with enough vocabulary to hopefully survive if necessary. I relished the fact that I was actively learning Portuguese *in Brazil*! I felt just a hint closer to the culture surrounding me, a smidge less "other." You could compare it to a first-time cooking experience. Sure, making a cake from a box isn't the same thing as being a chef, but it is the beginning of a cooking relationship. Here I was, creating something entirely new in an environment unlike anything I had experienced before. Now it was time to see how the pieces of me would fit into it and how they would be changed by it.

The leader of our expedition would be none other than Dr. Leandro Silveria. An expert on my favorite animal, Dr. Silveria is one of the world's foremost authorities on all things jaguar-related. Clearly, the man has an unwavering passion for his work, and having the opportunity to observe and support this commitment was an honor and an inspiration. The drive and devotion of environmentalists like him creates an incredible, positive energy that is infectious and validating to the spirit.

I have always believed in the eminence of nature, for she is the womb from which our existence springs forth—one that we share with all living things, whether animal or vegetable. During the previous ten years, my reverence for nature had been elevated through a variety of interactions with animals on Lake Roosevelt, along with a connection I felt when studying various Native American spiritual beliefs. I feel there is some truth in every religious practice or belief and that I am able to recognize what resonates with me from each discipline in order to walk a path that nurtures my spirituality. The result is my own personal growth, as well as the desire to better the world in which we all live.

Our expedition on the Araguaia River consisted of monitoring the corridors for signs of jaguar by way of scat collection with a trained dog. The research team included Dr. Silveria, his wife Dr. Anah Jacomo, PhD student Marian

Gregerini, the volunteers, and dog trainer Leo. Working with the dogs and their trainer was an amazing experience. The canines wear a bell around their necks and scout ahead of the group at about ten meters before circling back like a herding dog. When the dog sniffs out scat, it sits by the pile until the team arrives. A motionless dog means that his bell stops ringing, which signals to the researchers that the dog has found something that needs to be investigated. As a reward for a job well done, the dog then gets to enjoy some play time with his trainer. There are some specially trained dogs whose job it is to scout out the jaguar itself, as well.

Jaguars require a large range in which to hunt and mate. Looking for signs of other animal life is an additional method for identifying where they might be within that range. For example, the tapir is one of the big cat's favorite foods, so tracking that animal's hoof prints via GPS and monitoring its scat can help lead researchers to a jaguar. The jaguar's diet consists of 85 different species, which is an important aspect of maintaining the eco-balance in the range area.

Scat collection is an art form in itself. Members of the team must collect the findings, place it in jars with the appropriate solution, and send it off to the lab for identification. One becomes pretty good at identifying with the naked eye which poop comes from which animal. "And what do you do?" I mused in my mind. "I'm a professional pooper scooper!" There is actually a lot to learn about scat. For instance, ocelot and lynx scat have more skin or tissue residue from its prey than that of the jaguar. Also, if there is a lot of sign of ocelots or other cats in an area, then it is unlikely there will be any jaguars. Likewise, if jaguar scat is present, there's a good chance other cats will stay away from the area.

Our treks on land took us into the hills of the national forest and to unfamiliar and untraveled areas. Dr. Silveria led us down paths, up rocky hillsides, through dense bush, and into forested land. Because of the heat, we generally undertook these treks in the very early morning hours, tracking not only for jaguars, but also gaining insight to the predators in the area by way of signs of other wildlife.

In addition to these land treks, we also did a considerable amount of travel by water. The jaguar is not the only threatened or endangered animal in the area, and we were tasked with monitoring the pink river dolphin and the giant river otter, as well. We were keen to find signs of those creatures, of course, but also to monitor the environment and habitation of other life forms...specifically, humans. The impact of humankind was driven home when one realized that there were literally no sightings of pink river dolphins or jaguars in the areas with more homesteads.

The pink river dolphin's behavior is quite different from what comes to mind when most of us think of sea dolphins. Instead of being friendly and gregarious, these marine mammals are quiet and mysterious. You rarely see even the nose of a pink river dolphin, who surfaces silently, almost leisurely, to the top of the water, exposing only its blowhole. The animal gets its name from the pink color that is especially dark on their undersides. They have a somewhat prehistoric look to them with their pronounced spines.

Pink river dolphins live in small pods, usually of about five to eight members. They are graceful and tend to be more refined than their playful cousins. While you can hear them blowing off in the distance, the sound is devoid of the exuberant play and squeaking one expects from sea dolphins. It was a singularly soothing experience for Caroline and me to camp on the beach for a couple of nights, lulled by the rhythm of the water lapping on the shore, falling asleep and rising to the sound of the dolphins' breath.

While research involves the collection of numbers and other hard data, it also provides an opportunity to become an observer of life, to recognize the sameness that we share with other living beings. One afternoon I was privileged to watch as the river dolphins engaged in their version of activities that reflect the needs of all animals, including humans. As I stood on the beach next to a small inlet, four or five dolphins swam extremely close to me. The next thing I knew, they were jumping in and out of the water, causing quite a splash. In fact, that was their intention. The dolphins were churning up the shallow water to bring out the fish hiding at the bottom in order to have themselves a mid-day snack!

Shortly after this feeding frenzy, two other dolphins gave me a bit of a peep show as they courted one another near the shore. I stood just a few meters away in the cool water as they engaged in slow, graceful, alluring rolls with one another. It was breathtaking to witness, especially considering how shy and aloof these dolphins usually are. Yet there they were dancing with one another right in front of me!

Speaking of aloof, we never did see a single giant river otter. On the other hand, we did spy three smaller otters with their old-man moustaches and slick little bodies cutting through the water. The boating treks also provided a chance to see many caimans. While these scaly reptiles are considered "small" by crocodilian standards, it's easy for a person—say a tasty-looking American volunteer in a boat full of soft, naturally defenseless mammals—to imagine the kind of havoc they could wreak.

The sheer diversity of the animal kingdom is truly incredible, and just being introduced to new species was enough to create a shift within my spirit. Perhaps it could be better described as a broadening or a deepening. The more things I experienced, the bigger my soul became in order to encompass them all.

From the boat one day, I noticed a coatis getting a drink on the shore. These brown animals are long-legged and thin, and it brought to mind a raccoon but with a much longer, skinnier tail. I spotted him, and instantaneously my inner world, my awareness of reality, stretched. A capybara swam out of the river and scurried up the rocks, and with that, my brain created new synapses in order to record the event. When a toucan flies across the sky, it happens so quickly, but there is no mistaking what you are seeing; and at that moment, reality grows to encompass that animal's existence, the colors of his plumage, the sky in which he labors and glides.

The sky itself even seemed to become bigger within my own frame of reference. Often while on foot treks or driving around on the grounds, we would inadvertently startle flocks of green parakeets from the trees. Despite the fact that there were enough birds to transform everything into a momentary green flickering of light, they would quickly be engulfed by the enormity of the sky. At night the stars danced in paradox, being both billions of miles away and close enough to reach out and touch, to be gathered together like jewels that would never be allowed through customs and would have to be left behind in Brazil, carried instead within in my newly expanded consciousness.

Ahh, the warm, sultry nights of engaging conversation. Dr. Silveria continued to teach us each night after dinner. There were lessons on the jaguar, insights into difficulties with the ranchers, and light shed on many of the political policies that affected our work. It was not uncommon in the area for pretty much every cattle death to be blamed on the jaguar, so of course the ranchers wanted the jaguars gone. They saw the animals as a threat to both their finances and their way of life. The conservationists, on the other hand, were concerned with the jaguar's threatened status, as well as maintaining a healthy eco-system.

Both sides have been learning how to work together, based on trial and error. At first, ranchers were paid per head for any cattle killed, as long as they did not kill the jaguar in return. This got to be quite expensive, and a policy was put into place that mandated a carcass be examined for proof that the death was caused by a jaguar. It turned out that only a small percentage of the deaths were related to the jaguar. Some cattle were killed by other animals—sometimes a different cat species—some died of disease or drowning, and some were killed by a competing rancher.

An incredible amount of protecting the jaguar comes down to education. Ignorance costs so much more in the long run, but it is a tough barrier to break through. Ignorance, denial, and greed are the jaguar's enemies. They are the enemies of *all* endangered species, in fact. Even those who understand the animal's plight can be blinded, if the price is right. While on this expedition, there was a scandal that drew in Dr. Silveria that underscores this point.

A few years before, a very wealthy woman with strong ties to the community made a public pledge to support the doctor in his fight to save the jaguar. She made it clear that she was opposed to the killing of the animals, supporting instead the idea of finding ways to protect both them and the ranchers. However, during my expedition, a video surfaced that showed her interacting with a wealthy Russian as she allowed him to hunt jaguars on her property. Why did he hunt the jaguars? Simply for the sport of it. Why did she allow it? Because he paid her handsomely to do so.

Ignorance. Denial. Greed. And, perhaps we should add ego, too. I find it difficult to understand how people can be so removed from nature, to wrap my mind around how they can hunt and kill an animal that is near extinction, for nothing more than the thrill of it. Is this a sick extension of a person's own wounded ego? Is it a case of more money than sense?

Brazil is home to more than half of the jaguar's world population of 60,000. They are now extinct in two of the 21 countries they historically occupied—Uruguay and El Salvador. In the 1960s and '70s, approximately 18,000 jaguars were killed for sport and/or their coats each year. This destruction of the species has fueled the indignation and passion of people like Dr. Silveria and his wife Dr. Jacomo. Spending time with their operation, seeing their day-to-day lives and how they eat, breathe, and sleep the well-being of the jaguar opened my eyes beyond what I had already gleaned from reading books and articles or viewing documentaries. It was a world I had not experienced first-hand; and now that I had witnessed it, there was no un-seeing or un-learning what I had internalized.

There is a final enemy to add to that list: desperation. I was not surprised by the stories of corruption, but was certainly saddened by them. Two steps forward, one step back, right? My experience taught me, though, that most Brazilians *do* want what is best for their country, for the environment, for the planet. However, they feel like their hands are tied. Truth be told, this is the belief I came to hear in every country I visited during my journey. How, oh, how do you fight corruption when you have to focus the majority of your existence on merely feeding your family and keeping a roof over your head?

While my soul was expanding and my political whistle was being wet, I was also having a hell of a good time. Drs. Silveria and Jacomo were making arrangements and awaiting the arrival of a jaguar during my time with them, and it made for such excitement. The couple's home also encompassed a refuge for animals that had been neglected, abandoned, and abused by humans who attempted to raise them, as well as for those that were injured in the wild but could not be returned.

This particular wild jaguar had been hit by a vehicle and was originally thought to be dead. Really, though, it was in a state of shock. The Wild Land Service was transporting the animal by truck in hopes that Drs. Silveria and Jacomo could examine, rehabilitate, and release it back to the wild. The trip would take a few days, a stressful journey for wild animals who tend to become fragile when injured and placed in an unfamiliar environment.

I was one of three volunteers invited to the doctors' home and animal refuge for a few days' stay. In addition to the upcoming arrival of the injured jaguar, there were three orphaned six-month-old cubs that were being bottle fed. I had felt certain that the Universe was going to allow me an encounter with a jaguar, but never in my wildest dreams could I have imagined it playing out in this way. To know that I was going to interact with, to touch, my favorite animal—one that I could only have hoped to witness in a zoo—was truly an amazing and extraordinary gift. This was the animal that I had researched so thoroughly, the one that comes to me when I meditate, and the one that lured me to Brazil through my dreams. This was the animal that represents reclaiming one's power.

Oh, and *cubs*! Precious babies. Proof that there would be at least another generation of the animals we were working to save from extinction. It was overwhelming and perfect. Brazil was my leap of faith when it came to trusting my intuition and my spiritual beliefs. And here I was coming full circle.

The doctors' home was on the boarder of the Emos national forest. Along with their four-year-old son (appropriately nicknamed Jag), they lived in a beautiful hacienda on 10 acres of land. We were driven there by Marcondos, who was Anah's father and a very cute 70-year-old attorney who helped them out from time to time. As the volunteers arrived, we were greeted by a large red Macaw perched outside. The friendly pet followed us on foot to the veranda before flying up to light upon Caroline's shoulder.

Apparently he felt he had found a kindred spirit in Caroline as he set his powerful beak to work grooming her vividly dyed red hair. I emphasize the part about it being dyed, because it was not in the realm of the orangish hues sported by natural redheads. No, this was rubber-ball red. The Macaw contentedly worked his way through the thick mass of curls that fell to her mid-back. Like the bird's plumage, Caroline's hair was a distinct part of her identity, her trademark. To me, it represented the uniqueness that drew others to her. Caroline was such a delight, with her own way of looking at things, and the ability to make anything sound slightly posh with her accent, even when she was swearing about how she preferred the river dolphins to sea dolphins who she believes are "just too bloody squeaky happy!"

After we settled in that first day, the doctors told us about some of the other visitors they were expecting. A camera man would be joining us to shoot film for a BBC documentary about the young jaguar cubs and their plight. We would also be welcoming Lucy from Earthwatch who was a member of Dr. Silveria's team. She and her husband were bringing along a spider monkey that had been abandoned by its human family. Everyone was abuzz with anticipation of the filming and the new animals, as well as the excitement that surrounded the arrival of the injured jaguar a few days earlier.

Well, the ladies were excited. We volunteers had all earned nicknames during our adventure and liked to use them as often as possible. It was fun to imagine a brightly-colored comic strip featuring the Brazilian escapades of

Barbara Bush, Caroline the Caiman Catcher, and me, Jungle Jan. Greg, on the other hand, was less enthusiastic. He came along for the ride but really would have preferred to be out doing research.

Getting to know the wild jaguar was an experience that will remain with me for life. We needed to keep interaction with him brief to create as little stress as possible for the wary animal. I was bowled over by the intensity of the energy that these cats give off. His grace was undeniable, and he held a wild look in his eyes as he panted and exposed his fangs. I was both awed and intimidated by his presence. He absolutely radiated power. It was easy to see why the Mayans believed the jaguar was god-like and why they mimicked its behaviors and wore its tails and skulls during their most important ceremonies. At one point, the fierce predator looked at me and growled. Rather than being fearful, though I was elated that he acknowledged me. It was a special moment between two vastly different species, one that felt significant—well, on my end, anyway. I suspect it wasn't quite as momentous or life-changing for him.

Led by Dr. Silveria, the volunteers were given a tour of the property that was home to the refuge. There was so much to see and learn. At one point we were face-to-face with a sweet, playful, and gentle miniature deer called a Brocket deer. On the complete opposite side of the food chain, we were introduced to a relative of the jaguar. The jaguarondi is similar in appearance to a house cat but is a few sizes bigger. Both of the doctors care so much for the animals, and it was a wonder to witness it. At the time, they had a six-year-old female jaguar who seemed to be bonded to Dr. Silveria. She would get visibly excited to see him, and watching him speak to her in Portuguese as they worked together was truly endearing.

Of course, the moment of truth came when we were introduced to the cubs. The babies were so beautiful and as playful as kittens, yet already remarkably powerful at just six months of age. They could literally kill a human being who was unskilled in how to interact with them. It was a humbling experience to feel the incredible strength of their jaws while playing with them, knowing that a pair of long pants and some gloves were all that separated those razor-sharp claws from my ridiculously shred able skin.

Dr. Silveria walked the line between protecting our safety and that of the cubs. While he certainly did not want any of the volunteers to be harmed, he was also protective of his "babies." We were continually educated while spending time with the cats, with the doctor reminding us of just how dangerous the situation could become and how quickly that could happen. We were schooled in how to conduct ourselves around the cubs, as well as the appropriate way to handle them. Needless to say, I listened very intently.

The following morning, the camera man, who was named Rob, filmed the process of how a refuge animal is exposed to it new environment. The spider monkey had arrived and spent her first night in the crate in order to become familiar with the sounds and smells of her new home. Her crate included an opening that was large enough for ventilation and a bit of a view, but small enough that she could not pop a curious head through and get it stuck. When the time came to raise the front of the crate, everyone in the place was gathered around in anticipation of her reaction.

The crate itself was placed into a safe, enclosed rectangular area, approximately 20 meters in length. The lower two meters of the enclosure were comprised of a cement wall, with wire fencing stretching up and across the top. Barbara Bush, Caroline the Caiman Catcher, and Jungle Jan all watched breathlessly, anticipating a crazed monkey barreling out of the crate in search of sweet freedom. Instead, she made an entrance that would rival a ballerina stepping onstage before an expectant audience. She presented herself as a dignified creature full of grace and poise. She unfolded her long arms and legs like a flower blossoming and radiated a profound calmness that touched each of us like a gentle breeze. I gasped in disbelief.

This exquisite animal was about the size of a four-year-old and acted in many ways like a small human child. She approached Drs. Silveria and Jacomo sweetly and offered her hand. Annah accepted the small hand, petting it softly as she spoke sweetly to her new friend in Portuguese. It was, indeed, a precious, precious moment.

Her name became Lila, and everyone at the refuge fell in love with her. We had very little background about her, not even her age. Fortunately, it didn't appear that Lila had been mistreated by her former "owners," as she was very trusting and open to our embrace. Aside from a slightly runny nose, she appeared to be in good health. Lila would remain at the refuge for a while to ensure she was well, and then she would make a move to a zoo that was home to other spider monkeys. In the wild, they are very social creatures who live in large groups.

I awoke at sunrise the next morning and made my way to Lila's pen. Dr. Silveria was already there talking to her as one would to a new baby. His genuine love for animals was so plain to see in that moment. When he saw me, Dr. Silveria invited me into the enclosure with them. Lila walked right up to me and took my hand so we could take a little walk around the pen hand-in-hand. I was able to have the doctor take a few pictures of Lila and me together, and they are still a treasured keepsake. They remind me of how, as I sat to watch her swing gracefully around the pen as if she were child on a playground, she lowered herself down, walked over, and gave me a hug. Oh, my god, what a joyous feeling that was! It was so sweet and child-like and completely melted me.

Lila liked it when I scratched her chest. As she sat beside me, she slowly stretched herself out farther and farther in a not-so-subtle hint to scratch her belly, too. If I stopped, she would pick up my hand and place it on her torso where she wanted to be scratched. As Dr. Silveria was off tending to the other animals, Lila and I spent a tranquil morning lost in a camaraderie that transcended species.

Apparently she had a change of mood, however, when Caroline and Barb came visiting. They unlocked the pen and walked in slowly and quietly, just as we'd been instructed to do. Lila approached Caroline, took her hand, and sniffed it. Immediately, she threw Caroline's hand down and bolted to the other side of the pen. Poor Caroline was mortified, sniffing her own hand and finding no hint of soap or lotion smell there. We could not determine what had so offended the spider monkey.

Barb took a turn at trying to console Lila, approaching her while speaking soothing words. Lila was having none of it, however, and let out a monkey holler while trapeezing to the other side of the pen. Needless to say, the ladies were dismayed by Lila's behavior and were sad and disappointed not to have had a more positive experience with her. They were both honest in telling me that while they were a bit jealous, they were also really happy that Lila had shared such a nice time with me earlier.

That afternoon, a taxi arrived at the hacienda to take Greg to Goiania. As I walked onto the veranda, I saw him and the rest of the gang saying their goodbyes. Sitting off to the side was the taxi driver. When I saw his face, it was as if an invisible force hit me so hard in the stomach that it knocked all the air from me. I knew in an instant what this meant.

Back when I was still in the planning stages of my trip, Allen brought up the topic of me finding a lover on my trip. He was a bit of a romantic and felt that I should meet someone who could travel with and take care of me. Allen felt certain this would happen. I, on the other hand, was not. First of all, the purpose of my quest was to broaden myself, to have a spiritual adventure, not to find a man. I also knew that I didn't need anyone to take care of me.

Still, after this conversation, I began to have some inklings. They were cloudy images at first, but I recognized them as visions of people I would meet on my journey. I had shared with my friend Yvette about one of these visions, a dream I had of a dark skinned man with black hair that appeared in an aura. She asked, "Kinky hair? Is he African?" I told her that, no, his hair was jet black and pulled back. "I can only see him from behind, like he's walking away. I guess we shall see if it comes true."

At the time, I was still new at this vision thing and didn't know what to make of it. When I saw the taxi driver, however, the pieces clicked into place. I knew at that moment that I would certainly be meeting the man from my vision, and—like the taxi driver—he would be an Indigenous Indian. I began to feel a bit light-headed. I hadn't given that "vision" any thought at all since leaving on my quest, but when I saw the taxi driver, I definitely got hit in the gut. Clearly, I was getting closer to something big. I felt a bit off balance for the next couple of hours and ended up walking around the refuge to ground myself.

I needed to be focused, after all, because the next day I would be leaving all of this behind. I would say goodbye to the doctors, to my now closer-than-kin cohorts, and of course to Lila, the cubs, and all of the other animals at the refuge. As expected, the goodbyes were tearful. How I was going to miss my new English friends! After all, we made such an incredible team together.

I was the first to leave that morning. I was headed to the Pantanal, the world's largest wet ecosystem. It was home to hundreds of species of birds, as well as the jaguar. And, for a time, it would become home to me, as well.

CHAPTER 3
Brazil: The Pantanal

Most of the Pantanal lies in the state of Mato Grosso de Sol, with it extending into Moto Grosso, as well as portions of Bolivia and Paraguay. The wet season submerges 80% of the flood plains, with an average rainfall of 39-55 inches. The temperature in the Pantanal fluctuates from 32-104 degrees, with an average of 77 degrees. Each year, it would appear that the Pantanal is hopelessly doomed. Aside from river-dwelling predators and their hapless prey, what could possibly survive having its habitat entirely wiped out? Only the strongest trees could hold firm to the earth, and even the immovable rocks would be drowned and helpless below four feet of water.

And what would make its way to the surface? Whether stagnant pools or rushing rivers, you can imagine they would be clogged with the flotsam and jetsam of forest life. Old logs, rotting in the water and heat. The drowned carcasses of animals that couldn't shelter their way through the wet season would rise and sink, adding their own stench to the already heavy air.

In truth, however, this annual process develops into almost indescribable beauty. This perfect combination of moisture and warmth combines to nurture an astonishing biologically diverse collection of plants and supports an incredible array of animal species. It's estimated that there are 3,500 plant species, 1,000 different types of birds, 480 species of reptiles, 400 types of fish, 300 mammalians, and 9,000 different subspecies of invertebrates to be found in the Pantanal. Life, as they say, finds a way. And despite being razed to the ground each year, it rebuilds and transforms into something indescribably complex and beautiful.

The Pantanal does face considerable environmental threats, the most pressing of which comes from humankind in the form of commercial fishing and cattle ranching. Approximately 99% of the land is privately owned for the purpose of agriculture and ranching. There are 2,500 fazendoes (ranches) in the region with 8 million cattle. Erosion and sedimentation caused by this activity alter the soil and hydrological characteristics of the Pantanal. In short, many native species are threatened by the changes in important variables of the ecosystem. Hunting, poaching, and smuggling of endangered species add to this imbalance in the ecosystem, which is then exacerbated by deforestation.

A nnah had arranged a private taxi driver to escort me to Campo Grande, where I would stay overnight in a hotel before taking a chartered bus to the Pantanal. This taxi driver had transported many of the refuge's volunteers in the past, which made it feel like a somewhat safer mode of travel than the one-day ride by public bus. That said, I was clearly a foreigner, and a single woman traveling alone. If a quick glance wasn't enough to out me as a "gringa," certainly my broken, convoluted attempt at Portuguese was a dead giveaway.

My driver, Joe, was a short-statured Brazilian man whom I estimated to be in his early 60s. He was sweet and spunky and erroneously convinced that he could speak English. We had an entire day to fill, so we found ways to communicate, often centering entire conversations around a word or two that we could each understand in both languages. I clutched my Portuguese dictionary and gave it a thorough workout.

Joe and I bonded quickly as we drove through the green rolling hills and sugar cane plantations. I recognized him as a guardian angel sent to help me. He was not only my driver, he easily and without hesitation became my escort, protector, and guide as we wound our way through the rural areas of central Brazil. When we stopped in a small town to eat or stretch our legs, this wise widower made sure I knew how beautiful and unique I was with my light, curly hair and green eyes. He warned me that people would likely stare and that some would want to meet me.

He was not mistaken, either. When I entered a small

restaurant to take in some lunch in one of the towns along our route, the room grew unnaturally quiet. The customers' eyes followed me from the door to my seat. I caught the staff peeking at me through the kitchen door as I filled my plate from the buffet. Just as Joe said, some of them were intrigued enough to want to meet me.

For whatever cultural reason, it was usually men who sought me out. They would come directly to our table and introduce themselves. I was flattered, for sure, but I also found it endearing. I had gained some experience with this kind of curiosity during the jaguar expedition. While I would have thought nothing of seeing folks of different ethnicities at an amusement park back home, I was now living in rural South America. When Caroline and I spent one of our "play days" at a water park during that part of the research trip, our fair skin and unusual hair had drawn a lot of attention.

It's funny to be at an amusement park as a patron and suddenly find yourself filling the role of an attraction. Men and women would literally stop talking to stare at Caroline and me, unabashedly craning their necks to get a better view of the spectacle of us. Children walked right up to talk to us, sometimes touching us and then running away to tell their families all about their daring exploits.

In addition to our skin, hair, eyes, and accents, there was something else that made us stand out from the crowd on that day at the water park—our swimming attire. There's a reason that those thong-style bathing suits are called "Brazilian cut," after all. No matter a woman's size, age, or other factor, it was common practice for the ladies to wear what we would consider quite "skimpy" suits. Caroline and I were by no means prudes; we were just wearing what was normal to us, not to mention the fact that experience had taught me that better coverage on the bum led to less sticking on the way down the water slides. To that end, I was dressed in a halter-style one-piece suit with ample fabric in order to reach optimal speed. Caroline, who would make quite the picture with her flaming hair billowing behind her as she raced down the slides, had opted for a two-piece with a camisole-style top and brief-style bottoms.

When we climbed the flight of stairs to the top of the first slide, we found the attendant—an older man—completely up in arms, giving us the up-and-down elevator look. While we couldn't understand what he was saying in Portuguese, the tone of voice was pretty clear. Dr. Silveria was right behind us and spoke with the attendant, who was still quite flustered.

"What's the deal?" I asked the doctor. "It's about our swimsuits, isn't it? I don't get it…"

Dr. Silveria explained, "He doesn't think you're wearing swim suits. He thinks Caroline is in her underwear and you are wearing a dress and shouldn't go down the slide." Here we were in outfits that would have been fairly revealing back in our home countries, and we were being accused of wearing too many clothes! Fortunately, our mentor was able to explain to the attendant that styles of dress and what is appropriate vary depending on where you are in the world, and he eventually allowed us to hurl ourselves down the slides.

Despite being dressed in what was practically formal-wear, the rest of the day was spent fielding offers to come sit with others as well as being stared at by curious gawkers. I was also asked by many handsome young men to take a picture with them. After the quick Kodak moment, many of them would try to kiss me. Oh, my! This led me to the realization that any woman who is feeling a bit low about her appearance and is looking for a boost should go ahead and book herself a flight to Brazil!

My time with Joe the taxi driver helped to cement some of my earlier inklings about the way the Universe was choosing to care for and communicate with me. I was becoming more adept at noticing and interpreting the signs that had likely always been present, but undetected in my life. From dreams and visions, to "feelings" and coincidences that were so common they ceased to be coincidental, I found myself opening more and more to the possibilities and looking forward to them anxiously. It was my job to be prepared and open to accept the gifts that were being bestowed, and to accept them graciously.

On the surface, it would seem that Joe and I had nothing in common. Even our attempts at simple dialogue were thwarted by our linguistic limitations. However, we found a common language during our drive through the jungles. It was not something at all expected, but from this point on through my world travels I would discover that if the earth had a soundtrack, it would be full of Beatles songs. This older gentleman, this Catholic widower, this man who had lived a life so vastly different than mine shared my love for the Fab Four. I had uploaded much of their music onto my phone, and as we bumped along the long and winding roads of Brazil, we raised our voices together singing of Lucy and her diamonds, giving someone all our loving, and a psychedelic yellow submarine.

But not everything about Joe was unfamiliar. The Universe has an unbelievable sense of humor, and in this case, it meshed perfectly with mine. Many years before, I had been a fan of the sketch television show MADtv, and particularly of a recurring character named Stuart. Friends and I would often imitate this character, a five-year-old boy played by a grown man, by extending our arms out and shaking our hands side to side loosely while uttering is trademark phrase, "Doooon't let me do it!" With no knowledge of Stuart or the show, it turned out that this same gesture was a part of Joe's nonverbal repertoire. He would shake his hands at me in this same exact fashion to communicate "Shake a leg!" or "It's time to get going!"

Joe didn't know, of course, the reason I laughed so delightedly every time he tried to hurry me along in this way. Nor did he realize that this simple gesture helped me to feel comfortable and at peace in such foreign surroundings. I saw it as one of life's sweet little signs letting me know I was on the right track.

We arrived in Campo Grande early that evening, and I was taken to the home of one of Joe's friends. Francisco had his own travel agency and had created an itinerary for the next part of my journey. He did not speak much English, but his son and daughter-in-law were able to act as interpreters for us. Along with Joe, the group of us spent the evening in conversation. Francisco was a man of many talents, one of which was accompanying his own beautiful voice on the classical guitar. He was known in the area for his performances at a number of nightclubs, and I was treated to my own personal concert that night. He serenaded me in his own home with a bright, happy smile that radiated welcoming energy to his guest.

The entire family was so gracious and hospitable. They

were truly concerned for my comfort, that I was able to get where I needed to go, and that I was safe. It was abundantly clear that they were prepared to make these things happen. Somehow, I had traveled on an earthly plane but been delivered into a heavenly one that was populated with my own family of guardian angels.

During the course of the evening, I regaled them with tales from my adventure thus far. I also shared with them my continually-validated belief that the Universe was looking after me throughout my quest. The daughter-in-law listened intently and shared with me an experience where she and her husband had been watched over in a similar way. Two years earlier, they had planned a trip to Europe. Things were very busy at work, and she had put in many extra hours. On the eve of their trip, her boss called and begged her to stay just a few days longer. She relented and rescheduled her flight for later in the week. The next day they watched in horror as the evening news reported that the plane they had originally intended to take had exploded over the ocean.

She felt that their lives had been spared at the last moment. She and her husband did travel to Europe later that week, and when they returned from their five week vacation, they learned that their son had been conceived. While having a child is certainly a miracle in and of itself, he also became a daily reminder to them of how easily life can change and the forces outside of yourself that can affect that change.

I slept soundly that night, appreciating my lovely hotel in the bustling city of Campo Grande. Morning meant it was time to climb aboard the small charter bus that would take me to the wilds of the Pantanal. This was only the first leg of the journey, however, and upon arrival at the perimeter of the Pantanal, we unloaded from the charter bus and were separated according to the direction we would be traveling from there. My new mode of transportation was an old Chevy pickup truck. We adventurers climbed into the bed of the truck, taking seats on wooden benches with our belongings tucked beneath us.

There are two seasons in the Pantanal: the wet and the dry. It was May, and the wet season had just ended. During that time, the rivers had risen due to heavy rains, leaving nearly all of the Pantanal submerged in water. The roads and bridges were badly damaged or washed away altogether. This is how it is, year after year. We arrived at the very beginning of the dry season, when the roads and bridges were just becoming accessible—if they were there at all.

I suspect that the road leading us into the Pantanal was one of the most primitive, rugged stretches of road ever to be driven. The old truck ground its way through 25 kilometers of deep ruts, flooded-out bridges, and log-filled potholes that could have easily swallowed an entire car. The ruts were so deep, in fact, that there were times it felt that there were only two wheels on the ground. When we would come across truly unsafe bridges, we would all climb out of the truck to walk tentatively across the span before turning to hold our breath as we watched the vehicle slowly make its way across with all of our belongings on board. Would this be the one that snapped? Would this be the bridge that gave way, leaving us with no choice but to work together to push the truck out of the caiman infested river?

Our party was fortunate enough to stay out of the river, but we did experience technical difficulties, nonetheless. From time to time on our journey, the truck stalled out. The driver managed to coax the old hulk of a machine to within a reasonable distance of the eco-friendly hostel where we would be staying before telling us to abandon ship. Again, we climbed from the bed of the truck, this time taking our belongings with us and humping them down the road to our site. I was the only traveler who had opted for a backpack, and I sent up a little thanks as others struggled to get their luggage to its destination.

We were greeted there by our guide Sevi. Sevi was a nice looking Indigenous Indian, maybe in his early 30s. He was dark-skinned, well-toned, and had sparkling white teeth and a beautiful, ever-present smile. When he spoke English, it was with an unusual accent, one that I thought sounded like a pleasant mix of the many different accents I'd heard so far on my journey. At times it seemed Australian, at others English, and at other times still, it seemed to be influenced more by his native language. In truth, Sevi could converse in several languages. He was born to a dying tribe with only about 100 individuals left who could speak in their native tongue.

I wasn't so forward at first, but I eventually took to calling him Tarzan, which he accepted graciously. He had grown up with his tribe and had incredible knowledge. He could call the animals and they would respond back. It seemed that he knew every local plant and their medicinal uses. There wasn't a species of bird he couldn't identify. All of these skills came together to make him an excellent guide, always vigilant in watching for danger.

As our small group took to horseback one afternoon, my horse became nervous and jumpy. Sevi quickly spotted jaguar tracks and found part of a kill under the trees. In theory, I loved the idea of seeing a jaguar out in the wild, but I hoped not to do it while on the back of a terrified horse. Fortunately, I had Sevi to distract my thoughts. He was magnificent on his horse. In addition to being a skilled rider—having spent considerable time in the stables as a boy—he looked like he had ridden right off the cover of a romance novel in his chaps and cowboy hat, with his long, black hair blowing in the jungle breeze.

Upon arrival, Sevi gave the five of us a tour. The hostel was beautiful and well-kept, with the feel of a resort. There was a swimming pool, indoor and outdoor dining areas, a recreation room complete with billiards and ping-pong tables, and a seating area that offered access to the wide-screen TV. There was also a little outside bar called Lobo's, serving excellent caipirinhas. This is the national cocktail of Brazil, made with a sugar cane liquor and lime and was a treat I came to enjoy quite well. As I unpacked and got to know my small, private room, Sevi came to check on me twice to ensure that I was doing well and to see if I had any questions he could answer. We immediately developed a comfortable rapport, with him amiably poking a little fun at the foreigner. He even offered to help me with my Portuguese when I shared my interest in being better able to communicate during my travels. A tour guide with wit, intelligence, and a penchant for good customer service, I had hit the jackpot!

Our group dined together that first evening, sitting in the warm evening air while chatting and enjoying a drink. Sevi joined the conversation and shared with me that the resort had its own campground. "I love camping!" I told him enthusiastically, positively clueless that he might have any ulterior motive in mind. He responded with a similar level of enthusiasm, suggesting that he give me a personal tour of the grounds.

Even though it was near the full moon, the night was quite dark. It was a bit of a trek as we made our way to the campground with only a flashlight and Sevi's knowledge to guide us. My stomach was feeling somewhat prickly with nerves and excitement as we neared the beach where I knew the caimans resided. While it was certainly alluring and novel to be there at night, I found myself skeptical of the idea that I would ever feel comfortable tent camping in this particular place. Not to worry, I learned, as the resort also had an indoor facility for rent that included hammocks strung across the large room to keep campers from having to sleep on the ground.

Sevi and I sat on a bench together in what—despite my ongoing concern of being eaten alive by caimans—was likely the most romantic of moments in the history of romantic moments. The water lapped at the beach as we sat beneath a field of shooting stars that raced one another for the chance to carry my wishes off into the universe. We talked together for a while in that almost-too-perfect scene, when Sevi asked, "Do you want to go swimming?"

My thoughts immediately started racing. The first of them, which I kept to myself, was "Man, this guy works fast..." The next thought came directly on its heels and tumbled out of my mouth syllable by syllable: "Are you fucking nuts?!" I pointed out to him that I had only just arrived and that perhaps I would rather not spend my first evening as a midnight snack for the caiman and piranha that I knew lived in these waters. I used my arms to demonstrate the jaws of a caiman biting down in case he needed a visual to go along with my accusations that he was trying to get me killed. "I have plans and places to go, mister," I told him in a stern-ish voice. "My family would not be happy with me!"

Sevi laughed and said that we were too big for the caiman and that the fish were sleeping. He even pulled out that old trope of "They're more scared of you than you are of them."

"Whaaaaat?!" I exclaimed without irony. "They have much sharper teeth than we do!" At this point, I had begun to seriously consider that maybe this guy was a bit cuckoo, if you know what I'm saying. But, he continued on, reassuring me that the caimans are only aggressive when the waters are low or when it's mating season. He was so soothing as he explained to me that he had grown up swimming in these waters. He also let me know that it was okay with him if I didn't want to, but that he was certain we were safe from scaly predators.

I found myself starting to consider this obviously insane idea. After all, this could be part of my quest and would certainly be an opportunity to broaden myself. I double checked my thinking process. I had only had one drink that evening, and it was quite some time ago. The somewhat fuzzy edges of the bigger picture began to come into sharper focus as I realized why I had received such great "customer service" earlier in the day. Sevi was a guide, sure, but he was interested in giving me the "full tour."

"Okay. I'm in." There was no strong resolution in the words as I spoke them; rather, they came out the only way I could force them—as a near whisper. My internal voice was talking up a storm, however. Obviously, Sevi had swam here before, and the fact that he'd had this job for 18 years led me to believe he'd never actually gotten anyone killed. I sent out an urgent message to the Universe—perhaps more of a plea—asking for a sign that this was going to be okay.

We stripped down there on the beach. "You go first, but I'm right behind you," I called, adding as an afterthought, "Don't let me get eaten!" Sevi led the way. As I followed, the moonlight afforded me a view of his whole beautiful body from behind. His thick, shoulder-length hair was tied at his neck. His muscular back had been sculpted by nature and a lifetime of hard work. These details swirled together, and as I gazed upon this moonlit native, my jaw dropped and I froze.

At that moment, I recognized him. He was, without a shred of doubt, the man from my vision. The Universe had heard my plea months before I had rendered it. Emboldened with the knowing that I was exactly where I should be, I followed Sevi into the Paraguay River. We caught the current, let it carry us. Each time I heard a caiman splash and scamper away, I held my breath and pressed my bare body more closely to his. Perhaps this had been his cunning plan all along; perhaps it was simply nature conducting its symphony for our ears alone. Either way, I embraced the moment, just as I embraced the man—without hesitation, and with the understanding that it was a gift.

I ended up staying longer than expected at the resort. The typical guest would stay only three days, and it had been my intention to travel south for a few days to visit the fabled town of Bonito. It has a reputation as one of the most beautiful and environmentally pristine places on the planet. Special wet suits have to be worn to enter their waters. The Iguaçu Falls sounded fabulous, as well, but they were a very long bus trip away, and I wasn't all that confident in my ability to depend on my still very limited Portuguese.

The Universe intervened, however, and I found myself having trouble making arrangements for my excursion, both by telephone and Internet. I told Sevi, "I guess I'm not supposed to go to Bonito right now," interested in his reaction. "No," he said, "You are not. Stay another week then go south as opposed to going south for a few days and the heading back up this way." I had only two weeks left in Brazil and decided to listen to my inner voice and let my intuition guide me.

"Okay, I will stay and see what happens," I announced to Sevi and the rest of the staff at the hostel. Everyone seemed pleased by my decision. Many Brazilians live far from their families, working hard to send home money to support them. They will often work 16 hours a day, 7 days a week, going home to visit with their families for only a few days every couple of months. It was certainly a different way of doing things than I was used to; but it is their way of life, and they seem content with it. As a result, the staff looked to each other as a sort of surrogate family. I was adopted into this group, and despite sitting in the wilds of the Pantanal, I felt happy and safe.

I did struggle a bit when the parrots would wake me with their scratchy screeches each morning at five a.m. One would think that such undeniably beautiful creatures would have been endowed with a voice to match, but that was not the case. How, I would wonder with a pillow over my head, could something so gorgeous—practically a living rainbow—not be given a song to sing out across the rain forest that was more in line with its vibrant colors?

Brazil is home to one of the most diverse populations of birds in the entire planet. At least 1,901 species have been identified. Unfortunately, ten percent of these are threatened, including eighteen species of macaws. That number was 19 until recently, when another species went entirely extinct. Macaws are most well known for their bright plumage which Mother Nature has seen fit to combine in wonderful ways. Scarlet, yellow, and blue; bright green and red; blue and violet—there is practically no end to the combinations.

The Blue Hyacinth, a macaw, is the largest of all parrots, measuring up to a meter (3.3 feet) from the top of its head to the tip of its pointed tail, and it is also incredibly endangered. It is estimated that only about 2,500 of these rare birds survive in the wild. I was unaware of this fact at the time, and perhaps took for granted the fact that a flock of 15-20 perched in a tree just outside of my room at the hostel. They bedecked the jungle foliage like azure ornaments on a deciduous Christmas tree. In addition to its striking cobalt feathers and yellow-trimmed eyes, this bird also has the largest beak in its family. These are not the only features that make the Blue Hyacinth so rare, as unlike other animals, it can eat poisonous seeds and unripe fruit without harmful effects. The likeliest explanation for this is that the clay they pry from the riverbank to eat works as a detoxifier in their bodies.

In addition to illegal capture and sale of these animals, their existence is dangerously threatened by the palm oil trade. Macaws subsist on seeds, nuts, vegetable matter, and eight species of palm. The rainforests are clearly shrinking, with the manufacture of palm oil being one of the biggest reasons. Palm oil is used in as much as 50% of goods we use daily, including processed foods, candles, cosmetics, and bio fuel. The oil is extracted from the fruit's pulp, as well as from the seeds.

While I didn't necessarily love the screechy, squawky sounds of nature's alarm clock outside my sleeping quarters at daybreak each morning, it was certainly a blessing to be in that proximity to such rare creatures. Considering the Blue Hyacinth's diminishing population, it was an honor to behold not just one, but an entire tree full of them daily.

Being at the resort had the feeling of traveling the globe while in a stationary position. Travelers from all over the world passed through the hostel on their own grand adventures. Each had his or her own stories and experiences, and all were so generous in sharing them with me. I met Peter, a nurse from San Francisco—my old stomping grounds! We wiled away the hours talking about our favorite sites and places in the City by the Bay.

A few days were spent getting to know The Three Amigos. The three of them weren't actually traveling together, but I got to know them as a group and called each of them according to their geographical point of origin. Mr. London was an old soul at only the tender age of 24. He had been volunteering with wildlife organizations since he was a teenager. His goal was to become an environmental mediator between tribal communities and the State. I hung on his every word, rapt as Mr. London relayed story after story of his safari adventures.

Mr. Munich was a middle-aged man who wasn't entirely clear on what he did for a living. I got the impression that he did behind-the-scenes advertising work for a big television show in Germany. He was easy to talk to, and I felt comfortable with him almost immediately.

The third member of the group was Mr. Israel. This young gentleman had recently completed his mandated service in the Israeli army and had decided to continue his world travels. From him, I learned an incredible amount about the realities of Israel, rather than the media-spun versions that would have otherwise only come to me through the evening news back home. Had I traveled on to Bonito as planned, I certainly would have learned more about Brazil, but I would have missed out on these first-hand accounts of what life looks like all over the world.

As one of the longest-staying travelers at the resort, The Three Amigos asked me to lead them on a walk. They often joked about how "you practically live here," and it was true that I had more knowledge of the area than most of the other foreigners around us. As we left the hostel, I let them know that I had left my camera behind, which should ensure that something really great was going to happen.

We trekked together to the outer edge of the resort property. The landscape became thick and lush as plant life stretched to greet the early morning warmth. It was a peaceful, serene time of day, elevated by the birdsong that seemed to emanate from the greenery around us. The calm was broken by the intrusion of a rustling sound from a nearby bush. We stopped in our tracks in time to witness a huge anteater running out of the bush on its hind legs. Luckily, the animal was heading in the opposite direction as it dropped to all fours and scampered on its way. A large anteater can do as much damage to a person as a bear due to its sharp, powerful claws. They rarely attack, but will if they feel threatened or are protecting their young.

"See! I told you something cool would happen if I didn't bring my camera!" I shouted excitedly. The Three Amigos stood still as could be, and from the smiles on their faces, you would have thought they had just been to their first topless bar. Mr. London had been on several African excursions in the previous eight years but had never laid eyes on an anteater before that day. Mr. Munich and Mr. Israel stood speechless, their mouths hanging agape. They would later tell me that this experience was one of the biggest highlights of their entire trip. It turned out that in my case, it was just a taste of things to come.

Of course, these international experiences weren't the only thing keeping me occupied at the hostel. Sevi and I had stayed together in my cabin each night, him leaving at four a.m. to get to work. On a few occasions after a daytime excursion, we would sneak off to "his place"—a hut provided for employees for sleeping quarters.

He was, indeed, a sweet, tender lover. One night I found myself watching him sleep, his ebony hair laid out on my pillow, his perfectly toned body and beautiful dark skin sprawled confidently across my bed, and I was so consumed with the desire to photograph him in that moment that it took my breath away. I stopped myself, pretty sure that I couldn't blame lightning if the flash happened to wake him. I could just see myself stuttering and stammering, "Uh...it was a freak lightning storm. Yeah, that's it!"

It was a ridiculous thought, anyway, I told myself. Perhaps

almost as ridiculous as our age difference. I hadn't specifically asked him his age, but I knew he was much younger than I and probably a bit older than my own children. I didn't really feel particularly embarrassed by the number of years between us, though. Instead, it felt perfectly natural. There was such an easy flow to the reality of two consenting adults enjoying one another's company in the jungles of the Pantanal.

Before this journey, though? I would have never been able to imagine this scenario. I would have felt too self-conscious to even fantasize about a younger man, let alone to follow through on anything so torrid. But at this point, it was right. He'd come on to me, and I'd been given a sign of approval. There were other, younger women at the hostel, including a couple of German beauties that he could have pursued. I was not so naïve as to think he'd never done this before. He was young, hard working, and far away from his home town. It made sense that he would seek both comfort and pleasure where he could.

According to Sevi, he preferred older women. He claimed that when he was 18 he was married to a woman of 30. I held all that he said at arm's length, not unaware that he may well have been feeding me a line of malarkey, and not terribly concerned if he was. I was empowered by our liaison. I recognized that it was meant to be, and that it was temporary. I did, however, choose to enjoy the hell out of it while it lasted.

The sex was intimate, and while we didn't have many nights together, the ones we shared were long. His Indian heritage left his body without hair, making his skin almost unbearably soft and smooth. We would rest occasionally before entwining once again—our bodies in such stark contrast to one another, even in the dark: My freckled fair skin against his, as dark and sweet as Brazilian chocolate. My curly, short hair of strawberry opposing his long, jet black mane. My hands were small and soft, his were a working man's hands that could become gentle enough to caress me, to touch my arms, my abdomen, the curves of my hip; to send a shiver down the length of my spine.

I was living in each moment, not quite worshiping it, but definitely allowing myself to reside in it. I was free and liberated, and it was exquisite. Sevi was doting and sweet. His kisses were savory and passionate. Yet, when it was time for our four-a.m. farewells, we could part without undue concern. He would often kiss me in those last few minutes, and we would look forward to seeing each other in our official guest-and-guide capacity later in the day.

We had to sneak around like teenagers, which only added to the exhilaration. There was a "strict" policy of the staff not—you know—having sex with the guests. The policy, by the way, wasn't actually all that strict, as we were clearly not the only staff/guest pair to be doing the tango. There was a young Frenchman who had his sights set on one of the private female guides there with a Dutch couple. The guide did not acquiesce to his affections, much to the delight of the friendly receptionist who seized her opportunity and whisked the Frenchman off to her own bed.

There was another gentleman at the hostel who made no secret of his interest in me. Tony regularly declared that he was "in love" with me and occasionally left me both flattered and slightly uncomfortable as he tried to give me his prized possessions. While he was kind and generous with his praise of my beauty, I was not interested in his advances. Besides, I was busy enough having my own secret affair with Sevi.

While sexually satisfied, I found myself deprived of sleep, which may have played in to the fact that after my first week at the resort, I began to get emotional. I trekked back down to the beach where Sevi and I had sat under the stars and splashed with the caimans on my first night at the hostel. The enormity of my time in Brazil started to settle within me enough for me to recognize how much had truly happened. I had spent time with the jaguars, befriended a spider monkey, drank and supped with folks from around the globe. I had trekked into the Pantanal and been overwhelmingly welcomed and accepted by the kindhearted people around me.

And, once again, my existence expanded. All of these experiences were now a part of my being. And I felt so damned GRATEFUL for it all. I was grateful for these gifts. I was grateful for the spiritual opening that allowed me to begin to see them. I was learning to trust my intuition, to see signs that had likely always been before me but that I had overlooked. Not unlike the trees of the Pantanal in the wet season, I had been uprooted. Not unlike the immovable rocks on the forest floor, I had been submerged. But, like the jungle, the torrential rains had given rise to a new existence within me. I was still the same person I had always been, but I was more.

I put on my headphones and danced to John Mellencamp singing, "Your time is now to do what you must do. And in this moment..." This was my song. It summed up my feelings perfectly on what I felt was a perfect day. At that moment, I knew I had ARRIVED. I had traveled to

Brazil all on my own. I went there to meet the jaguar and found her within myself. I danced and sang in jubilation. I cried sparkling tears of joy as I stood on the beach while the caimans watched from the opposite bank. They offered no commentary as this curly-haired white woman gyrated across the sand.

Early one evening, Sevi took me on a walk, saying that he wanted to show me something he never tired of looking at. We made our way through a patch of lush mosquito-infested jungle before coming into an open field. The grass came up to my waist, but being only 5' 1 ½", the terrain probably seemed much deeper and rougher to me than it would have to someone less vertically challenged. Sevi pointed me to the west where the setting sun was lighting the sky aflame with vibrant orange and red hues.

The star that is the center of our solar system was set against a sky so large that it seemed as if we were on the edge of the planet. If we just took a few steps forward, we could peek down over the side and reveal all the mysteries hidden there. As I gazed ahead and absorbed both the view and the last rays of light for the day, I saw what looked like a black line moving from the horizon towards us. As it approached, Sevi took my hand and whispered, "Here it comes."

The black line stretched across the wide open space and flickered. It was made of hundreds upon hundreds of birds growing more distinct as their travels brought them closer. Sevi explained that every evening, just when the sun sinks below the horizon, these birds rise up and fly east to rest for the night. And each morning, at the first sign of daylight, they migrate west again. Twice a day for ten minutes or so, the sky above this particular area of open space was beauty in motion. I held my breath as the birds approached and then smiled with the awe of a child as our paths briefly intersected. The birds glided quietly, slowly, with perfect rhythm and synchronization of their wings across the sky. The sound was no more than that of a light breeze, and if one hadn't happened to look up at precisely the right time, it would go completely unnoticed. Nature granted an unparalleled performance of grace and elegance for everyone and no one.

A few days before I was scheduled to leave, Sevi was called into town for a meeting with the owner of the resort. We feared that he was being summoned because of our relationship. I watched as he climbed into a truck filled with travelers who were off on the next legs of their adventures, but not before giving me a hug and kiss right out in the open—in front of staff and patrons alike. He said he would return in a day. I never saw him again.

Tony, the staff member who had repeatedly professed to be "in love" with me, seemed ready to fill Sevi's shoes, suddenly finding it unbearable to be away from my side. I was not interested in his advances and was fairly uncomfortable with the attention he paid to me over the next few days.

The staff of the resort graciously threw me a going-away party the night before I was to leave. I had been there for 12 days and would be heading out in the morning with a French family that had been traveling the world for a year. At the party, I inquired about Sevi and asked the others to extend my thanks to him for being my guide. I thought I noticed eyes shifting quickly to one another as they mumbled something about not being sure if they would be able to do that. After a bit of digging, I learned that Tony was Sevi's supervisor. Tony had suspicions about our relationship, and after observing the Sevi and me while watching a football game with a group of staff and patrons, he had interrogated the younger man. Apparently, he didn't like the answers he got, and Sevi was called away a few days later. I felt blindsided by this realization, although in retrospect, I probably should have put two and two together.

There was absolutely nothing I could do about the situation at that point. While I wanted more answers and would have liked to have had a proper goodbye, there didn't seem to be a lot of sense in pursuing the situation. What would happen if I found Sevi? Neither of us was looking for more than what we had, and while we shared something special, there was little or nothing that could be accomplished by tracking him down.

The entire party was bittersweet, of course, but I chose to enjoy my last night at the resort. The next morning the French family and I headed off, and I was finally able to visit the Iguaçu Falls. They are larger than either Niagra or Victoria Falls, and—to hear the locals tell it—far more spectacular. Mr. London and a few other travelers had encouraged me to go there instead of Bonito. He promised that I had to experience the falls. "There is nothing else like it. You feel it, and it changes you." Considering the travels of this worldly young man, it seemed clear that he would know what he was talking about.

It actually took 26 hours of bus rides to reach the falls, as we had to make a side trip to Campo Grande to buy the right tickets and then backtrack and travel even farther south to the border of Brazil and Argentina. It was hard to wrap my brain around the fact that I actually had to travel backward to get where I was going, but the ticketing system was primitive. There was no option to go online and purchase a ticket to the falls, no way to pay by phone. The only option was to purchase the ticket in person at the bus station. Unfortunately for me, the bus station in question was in completely the wrong direction. I literally had to take a bus to get a ticket to take a bus.

If someone were to ask me if it was worth it, though, I would answer "yes" and tell them that I'd do it again in a heartbeat! It was truly one of the most powerful environmental experiences of my life. The area includes 275 individual waterfalls, with more water than I could imagine, even after standing before them and seeing it with my own eyes.

The theory is that the profound effect of the falls may be the result of the ions produced by the falling, churning water. Just as Mr. London said, I felt changed. During my visit, I was able to view the falls from the water below, from paths that ran alongside them, and from observation platforms where the roaring of the water was almost deafening. In that place, my heart and soul were happy with no effort on my part. I could see why it was considered a sacred place and could almost imagine contentedly giving myself up as a sacrificial offering. Luckily, no one was asking for that kind of commitment.

During the few days I spent at the Iguaçu Falls, I had many opportunities to continue to expand my existence, to run far and away over boundaries that I would have previously allowed to limit my experience. My physical, mental, and spiritual abilities were all tested as I conquered a tree-top obstacle course, sped along a zipline, climbed a rock wall, went white water rafting, and repelled myself down a 50 meter tower overlooking the falls. The last of these was particularly momentous, as I have lived with an ongoing fear of heights. As the saying goes, it wasn't the fall that worried me, but the landing! As I made my way slowly down the tower, I was so distanced from my fear, however, that I actually found myself contemplating how amazing it would be to take pictures of the birds from that vantage point.

Visiting the Iguaçu Falls made for the perfect capstone experience for my time in Brazil. It allowed me to reflect on the previous weeks. The soothing effect of the water, or the ions, or whatever the heck led to such a feeling of well-being provided the sense of calm I needed to integrate my new awareness of the world. I absorbed these changes physically, emotionally, and spiritually. I was stronger, more confident, and ready to see what my quest held in store for me next.

CHAPTER 4
Joplin, Missouri

During my time in South America, I grew accustomed to the lushness and vigor of the jungle. Everywhere I traveled was teaming with life, vibrating with an energy that was contradictorily frenetic and soothing at the same time. What came next in my journey stood in stark contrast to that and would expand my awareness in completely new ways.

I had intended to spend a week in Mexico for a brief respite before continuing my animal-related adventures, but before I left the Pantanal, I received news of a catastrophic event. The city of Joplin, Missouri had been devastated by a tornado so massive that at times it stretched as much as a mile across. The destruction it left in its wake was horrific.

My friend Martha Lynn worked in Joplin and resided just outside of the area in Neosho, Missouri. I had visited her a few years prior, so I had some familiarity with the town of Joplin. Martha Lynn and I felt that perhaps my experience as a psychiatric nurse could make me a valuable volunteer in the aftermath. I had so far been accepting so many gifts bestowed upon me, and it seemed fitting and right that I would reroute myself to Missouri, via a short visit home to Washington, and do my damndest to give back whatever I could. My days of jaguars in the jungle and Beatles in Brazil had come to a close, and I made my way to Joplin to provide whatever assistance I could for the next week.

The visit home was a speedy one, but I recognized the need for some self care. I had asked a lot of my body in South America, and getting a massage was high on my list of things to do. I was somewhat travel-weary, and both my body and my mind would benefit from an appointment with my massage therapist, David. He and I swapped stories back and forth during the treatment, me sharing the highlights of my trip, him catching me up on the goings on of his family.

David was interested to hear that I would soon be heading to Joplin. He said that another of his clients had a son volunteering there through AmeriCorps, most likely doing tree removal. While tree removal doesn't seem all that unusual after a storm (those things blow over, right?), this young man would probably be removing trees from areas that normally wouldn't have them, such as the middle of streets, the interiors of buildings, and so on. This was my first hint that things in Joplin would likely be outside the realm of what I expected.

Martha Lynn retrieved me from my flight into Kansas City on a Friday evening. The following morning, we made the several hour trip back to Neosho, and she filled me in on the realities of the tornado. Due to its unusually large size, it had moved slower than most tornados. Men, women, and children watched in awe and disbelief as what appeared to be a black wall advanced, literally sucking up everything in its path, rending it apart, and then spitting it back out in unrecognizable form. The tornado was ranked an EF5, the most powerful of storms, with winds blowing more than 200 miles an hour and peaking at 250.

As we drove through Joplin, I could barely comprehend what I saw. Although the storm had passed nearly a month before, it looked to me as if it had merely been yesterday. Half of the city was flattened for miles, with the horizon broken by standing bathrooms. As the tornado came through, it demolished homes but often left the bathroom doorways intact. What had once been a rarely-considered part of a house's interior now remained as the only identifiable part of a family's home. The doorways framed the devastation, their silhouettes leaving one feeling as if they were standing amidst the ancient ruins of a city that had fallen in an unwinnable war.

Tall buildings had been reduced to piles of rubble, and I grappled with the fact that people had been living their everyday lives in these facilities as they fell. It had been a Sunday afternoon in May, with folks going about their business. They were shopping at the grocery store for the upcoming week, standing in line at Home Depot to purchase items for yard projects, or grinding out a shift at the local fast-food place where they worked. People were driving around to finish up their errands—returning a borrowed tool, picking up postage stamps, getting kids home after a sleepover at a friend's. Families who had attended church that morning were now preparing dinner. It was a typical day for most of Joplin.

For some, it was even a special day. The senior class and their proud parents were attending their graduation ceremony. The class had been larger than usual that year, so the event was moved to a site three miles north, a change that would possibly save hundreds of lives, as the high school itself was directly in the tornado's path and was completely demolished.

Throughout my first day and those that followed, Martha Lynn and others shared their stories of the tragedy. These were recountings of people trapped beneath collapsed buildings, unsure of whether they would ever be found; of those impaled by debris flying through the air at hundreds of miles per hour; of human beings who were sucked into the whirling beast at home or at work, only to be found in a completely different part of town. Even a few miles away, the tornado created such strong winds that pedestrians and vehicles alike were pulled, sliding against their will across parking lots and walkways.

Of course, there were also many stories of people going to heroic lengths during and after the storm. I was told of a Pizza Hut employee who helped terrified citizens run into his restaurant for safety. As he tried to protect them by holding the door closed against the winds, he was ripped away. Neighbors dug through rubble to save each other from suffocation and being crushed to death.

Emergency personnel from nearby towns made their way quickly to the area. As citizens clawed their way out from under their collapsed homes or places of work, they immediately banded together to clear the streets in order to provide access to emergency vehicles. Individuals used their personal vehicles to gather up and transport the injured. The National Guard arrived within 45 minutes from the moment the tornado touched ground.

The death toll that day reached 158. Despite the warning sirens, many of the townspeople were caught off guard. At that time of year, the sirens sounded daily, no matter the size or relative proximity of the tornado. It was a bit of a nuisance, but it was nice to know that the sirens were there should the "big one" come along. Most people assumed that this warning was like all of the others, and many told me about how they just kept right on with their business for several minutes before it finally registered that the sirens still had not stopped.

The giant gray force injured 1,150 people and ranks as one of the U.S.'s deadliest tornados, not to mention the most expensive one in the nation's history. People who had been previously waiting at a red light found their cars being blown around as if they were on a skating rink that had tilted. Others were sucked into the storm and tossed back out like kernels of corn in a hot air popper. Large trucks were found wrapped around treetops, and all of the trees themselves had been stripped of bark—not by the tornado itself, but just by the winds that accompanied it.

For more than 22 miles, the swirling monster devoured everything in its path. Neighborhoods were flattened as far as the eye could see, houses ripped off their foundations. Some were left behind in splinters; others were swept away completely. St. John's Medical Center, one of the biggest buildings in Joplin, was hit so hard that it shifted four inches off of its foundation. The hospital's windows blew in, and staff members placed their own bodies over those of patients to try and shield them from glass, debris, and flying medical equipment. Not all were successful, and the hospital saw six fatalities.

The reality of surviving the aftermath of a tornado is much different than what I would have thought. When these types of natural disasters are reported on the news, I usually thought of things like the need for food and water, maybe some blankets and clothing, perhaps some hot coffee for volunteers helping with cleanup. I almost have to laugh at my own naivety.

Imagine the emergency workers arriving and finding no street signs to navigate by. In fact, because of the debris, it was often impossible to physically locate the street. Even those who had been lifelong residents of Joplin could offer little help, as landmarks they had grown accustomed to using were simply gone. A person would crawl out the pile of timbers and brick that used to be their home and not even be able to identify which direction was north or south.

This sense of disorientation was aggravated, too, by the fact that so many people were in shock. Everything they knew had vanished in minutes, replaced by what would likely have been their previous description of hell. And amongst the ruin were bodies. Some of the bodies were screaming. Some were moaning. Others were horrifyingly quiet and still.

The hospital staff was inundated, and again, things that I would have never thought of simply became reality for them. A surgical team was in the O.R. operating on a patient when the storm hit. They found themselves in the dark with no power, the room filling with water from a broken pipe. While you might think that lack of water is a big problem in a natural disaster, the abundance of it from various sources can actually be a bigger threat. They finished the surgery in rising water by flashlight. Despite not knowing where their own families were due to a lack of phones, Internet connections, and other means of communication, these healthcare professionals saved life after life.

Many of them injured, shocked, and confused themselves, the medical staff stayed and triaged hundreds of incoming patients who arrived on foot, in vehicles, and in the arms of loved ones who had carried them untold distances in search of help. They also evacuated 183 patients, along with supplies and equipment, to an emergency triage center. The wounded would continue to arrive, impaled with boards, steel, and glass, and with broken and lost limbs. In addition to these more obvious injuries, many people had been badly burned due to broken hot water pipes when hiding in their bathtubs. The medical professionals, many of whom eventually succumbed to post traumatic stress disorder as a result of their selflessness, worked tirelessly to save others.

As I said, I arrived about a month after the actual event. There were many in-state medical professionals involved in caring for the townspeople's physical and mental health, so it was determined that despite my medical knowledge, I would focus my efforts toward the cleanup. That Monday, I walked into the volunteers' station and gathered my safety equipment: a helmet, masks, and goggles, and loaded onto a bus. We were given instruction on how to sort debris. Wood went in one stack, metal in another. There were piles for clothing, appliances, greenery, and more.

Another of the unexpected aspects of a tornado's aftermath is the fact that the air can literally become toxic. Chemical agents are one thing, but all of the swirling wind and violence stirs up natural dangers, such as spores. This was an ongoing difficulty from day one, as spores would settle into people's open wounds, compounding the injuries and fostering horrible infections. Unfortunately, this added to the death toll.

The volunteers were transported to the high school and then formed into groups led by one of four Americorps members. These leaders stood out in their army green uniforms, which was helpful in spotting them when out in the field. The newly-formed teams loaded onto another bus and we were taken to our designated neighborhoods. We invaded them like an army of ants, dutifully marching back and forth, carrying away everything in our path.

My neighborhood on that first day was up on a slight hill, affording me a disturbing panoramic view. The high school was to the west, and the remains of the city were on the east. The "city" was a wasteland of timber. Foundations gaped with no houses to support. Rooftops lay on the ground. A few suffering trees attempted vainly to hold on to life. My mind reeled and my guts wrenched within me.

As much as I felt like I knew what "disturbing" and "gut wrenching" meant at that moment, those feelings would be taken to a whole new level with my next task. I covered my face with the mask and goggles and got to work sorting through other people's personal possessions. I did not know the people whose homes I was categorizing into piles that would be hauled off to be disposed of or recycled. I didn't know their stories, their histories, their loves and losses. I didn't even know if they had made it through the tornado alive. Each item likely held some significance to another person, and he or she would never see it again. Maybe the dress I put in the clothing pile was worn to an anniversary date. Perhaps that shattered glass had spent years protecting a family portrait.

The mood among the volunteers was solemn and quiet. There was so much debris that I wondered how we would ever get through a single house, let alone the entire neighborhood. The best I could do was trust that a system had been established to get the work done. We were an assembly line that produced tangible proof that progress was being made, however slowly.

It wasn't until we dug in that I realized how many layers there were to the stacks of rubble. While there are the obvious household items like furniture and shampoo and kitchenware, there were many hazards: pesticides in the garage, bathroom cleaners, unsteady tree limbs. Firearms and ammunition were mixed in with toys and roof shingles, and when these things were found, we would have to pause so that a SWAT team could be called in for safe removal. Metal fencing was wrapped around what was left of buildings. And so very much of what we touched was broken, jagged, and sharp.

My eyes landed on a photograph amid the wreckage of that first house. It was a picture of children in their pajamas, posing in front of a Christmas tree. I prayed that they were okay. My mind couldn't help but wonder about their lives, where they were when the tornado struck, and if they survived. "Thank God it isn't me and my family." The thought came, unbidden, and I felt ashamed of myself for a moment. Really, though, that was probably the very reason that so many of the thousands of volunteers were there. Because we were okay. Because our families were intact. Because we were abundantly grateful that it wasn't us.

Those volunteers came from all over the country to bring whatever help they could provide. A couple that happened to be driving through on their honeymoon stopped to help for a day. A young fisherman traveling from Texas to Alaska stayed a week. A young man from New York who had absolutely no connection to the area or its residents felt overwhelmingly compelled to be a part of the recovery, and so he came. Church groups from Missouri and other nearby states set up an outdoor kitchen in the high school parking lot where they cooked, served, greeted, and supported all the volunteers who came through their line.

The bus picked us back up at noon for lunch. The church folk provided us with barbequed chicken, burgers, and hot dogs; sandwiches; and all of the side dishes you might expect at an outdoor gathering.

Rather than taking the bus back to my neighborhood, I decided to hike the distance. I was grateful that the weather had unexpectedly cooled. The previous week it was in the 90s and humid, but the temperature had dropped to the high 80s with a slight breeze. When I got to the site, I stopped at an ice chest to grab a cold bottle of water. A young man in one of those green Americorps uniforms offered to get me one.

"Where are you from?" he asked. This is pretty typical small talk, considering that the volunteers hailed from all over the U.S.

"Spokane, Washington," I replied.

He looked at me a little funny and repeated the words

back to me in a disbelieving, sarcastic tone, "Spokane, Washington?" His response made it seem as if I had told him I came from Mars. I was up for a little sparring, and put my free hand on my hip in a gesture of defiance.

"Yeah!" I said. "Spokane, Washington. What's wrong with that?!"

It was my turn for disbelief, though, when he laughed and said, "I thought you were joking; that someone had put you up to this. *I'm* from Spokane!" We laughed and hooted a bit, giving each other a big hug as if we were long-lost siblings reunited at last. The other volunteers that had arrived back from lunch looked at us in amazement. This was the first time all day that any joy had been expressed.

The two of us smiled and reminisced about home. It turned out that he graduated from the same high school as my son, but he didn't recognize the name. Then we learned that we came from the same neighborhood. My voice was getting higher and higher in my excitement over these revelations. We chatted about familiar landmarks back home before he extended his hand and asked my name. I introduce myself and about fell over when he said, "I'm Matthew Christenson."

The words somersaulted over each other in their eagerness to make their way out of my mouth. Did his mother see a massage therapist named David on the South Hill? Matthew answered, "Yes." Once again, I started jumping up and down.

"I can't believe it! I think you're the person David was telling me about last week!"

Matthew explained that after a month in Joplin, this was his last day. It certainly felt like serendipity. His last day, my first. A reason to smile and be joyful amidst the anguish of the day's duties. A touch of home to remind me that my city, my home, my relationships were still intact. I gratefully accepted this sign from the Universe that I was in the right place at the right time.

To drive it home, though, there was yet another validation on its way. A crew was in town filming a story about Americorps, and they asked to include the story of Matthew's and my meeting. I was thrilled—but at this point not entirely surprised—to discover that one of the cameramen was a 1st generation Greek-American. We spent some time talking about my upcoming trip to Greece, and he offered me some insight into what to expect. It seemed that no matter where I went in the world, I was always being prepared for what would be coming soon.

I left the cleanup early on two different days in order to volunteer my efforts toward another often overlooked reality of natural disaster relief. The storm hadn't only affected humans, but had also caused trauma to all manner of animals. Literally thousands of pets and livestock had been lost and injured during the tornado. Entire warehouses had been donated in order to house and care for those that had survived.

Anyone who has ever had a pet dog greet them as they arrive home from work knows that animals have feelings. They get happy, sad, excited, and lonely. The animals of Joplin were no exception. These cats, dogs, horses, cows, and more had been through a truly traumatic experience.

They suffered major injuries and were separated from everything and everyone they had ever known. They were in a strange place, surrounded by unfamiliar animals that were also struggling.

They were nervous and depressed. They were hurt and frightened. And, they relied on volunteers for their every basic need. Imagine the amount of food that it takes on a daily basis to keep thousands of stranded animals alive. Volunteers worked around the clock to care for wounds, keep cages clean, and provide as much comfort as possible to these scared, confused animals.

I did my best to help in any way possible. I washed thousands of dishes and followed the team leaders' instructions. I offered words of comfort and hugs to displaced pets and volunteers alike. My purpose for having started my adventure had been to help animals, after all. While the original focus had been to engage in work to protect and preserve endangered animals like the jaguar and rhinoceros, the Universe seemed to have taken it upon itself to show me that there is peril for all animals—not the least of which is the human animal. While we represent the greatest threat to other life on the planet, it's a good idea to remember that we are still at nature's mercy.

The people of Joplin were heartbreakingly appreciative of the hard work being done by the volunteers. Everywhere we went, as soon as it was discovered we were from out of town, the gratitude would flood toward us. Every person, no matter how they had personally been affected by the tornado, would thank us and thank us and thanks us. There were banners strung all over town with the words "Thank You, Volunteers" providing a visual reminder of the gratitude when there weren't townspeople offering it aloud.

When you hear the phrase "salt of the earth," the speaker is talking about people like these. Joplin was full of hard-working folks who were grounded in reality long before the tornado ever came. I noticed it on my previous visit to the area a few years before. Visiting Joplin had been a bit like going back in time. People there lived out their traditional old values, which became even more apparent when one saw the literal interpretation of "neighbor helping neighbor."

Most of the people wanted to rebuild their lives in Joplin. There is no irony in saying that they would have to do so from the ground up, as it would entail the actual rebuilding of homes, businesses, and roads. The infrastructure would also require either extensive repairs or all-new construction. Everything from plumbing and electricity to phones and Internet service would need to be rebuilt. Traffic lights, street lights, emergency services, barns and garages, the replanting of crops—there was not an area of life that didn't need a reboot.

Even people's own histories would likely need to be reconstructed. Who knows what drivers and vehicles were licensed once the DMV was destroyed? How do you repli-cate the students' entire academic history when the schools' records were wiped out? Even if the pharmacies hadn't run out of medications, there was no access to customers' medi-cal histories. The effort would take more than rebuilding a town—it would require rebuilding entire lives.

A few of Joplin's residents were not interested in rebuilding, feeling they needed a fresh start somewhere new. It was impossible to blame them for feeling this way. Nearly everything they knew was gone, and whatever was left would be an ongoing reminder of that day. The dread of a future tornado also hung over many of them, and they needed to be released from that fear—even if it meant moving themselves and their families far away. They'd already been literally uprooted, and for them it was time to do so figuratively, as well.

There were still other individuals who seemed to be caught somewhere in between. When I dropped Martha Lynn off at work one day, I met one of these haunted, in-between people. He was a retired U.S. Marine who was on his first day back since the storm. His face had the unmistakable look of someone suffering from PTSD—he was clearly rocked by sadness and loss. Here was a man who had been prepared to go to war for his country, who had trained as an elite, and who had selflessly served to protect the lives of those in Joplin and far beyond; and he was utterly crushed by hopelessness in the face of what had happened here. "No way," he said. "I'm done."

By the third or fourth day, my own fatigue was settling in. The work was physically demanding and emotionally draining. I realized that outside of childbirth, I had never been so utterly exhausted in my life. On this afternoon, I simply plopped myself down in a local park, not really up to going any further.

A gentleman happened by and offered to drive me to my next destination. Apparently volunteerism was in his genes, as he shared with me that his daughter was currently working at an orphanage in Nairobi. I perked up a bit when

I heard this and exclaimed that I was going to be in Nairobi in July. He shared with me some of his daughter's experiences, and once again I found myself marveling at how things seemed to line up and give me faith that I was moving in the right directions.

My aversion to really listening to the voice of the Universe had been more or less stripped away at this point. I had already experienced so many manifested visions and impossible introductions and more-than-I-hoped-for dreams come true. I was fully invested in my experience and redoubled my efforts to actively watch for signs rather than just noticing them in retrospect.

As my time in Joplin came to an end, I took with me more than memories or a sense of having made an effort to help others. I also had a new insight into how truly hard life can be when circumstances are shaped by forces so far outside of your own control. In this case, the contributing factor was a tornado; but I would soon see how so many other difficulties can hijack one's opportunities and undermine plans for the future. In the next few months, I would get an even closer look at the realities of the third world, where poverty, gender inequity, and "the way things have always been" are an EF5 tornado whose winds blow for entire lifetimes without pause.

But, just as I found in Joplin, I would come to see that the ability to go on, to make due, even to be happy despite enormous hardship would appear to be a universal human trait.

CHAPTER 5

Greece

The Amurakikus Gulf has been home to one of the highest densities of bottleneck dolphins in the Mediterranean area. Unfortunately, it is also barely hanging on to its existence. There are about 150 of these marine mammals in the Gulf, a tragic decline from the thousands that were found there in the 1990s.

There are plenty of threats to the dolphins, but the largest by far has been the practice of trawling by larger fisheries. The giant trawlers are thrown overboard where they sink to the ocean floor. They are then dragged by the boat, scraping up everything in their path. Nothing is safe from the trawlers, as they rake up plants, marine life, rocks, shells, and coral. There are entire dead spots in the ocean floor where life has simply been scraped out of existence.

The threat from trawling cannot be overstated. It has been estimated that life in the ocean could be devastated in as little as 40 years due to this practice. Not only does it destroy whatever it comes across by scrapping the ocean floor, it's size up to 330 feet wide and over three stories high, but the effects of the damage ripple out, not unlike the wake of the boat above. There are thousands of these everyday on the bottom of our sea beds around the world. The trawlers kill the fish and other food sources, which in turn means there isn't enough to support the dolphin population. The loss of feeding opportunities also affect the sea bird population. It takes life to sustain life. Healthy development, whether of a person, an ecosystem, or an entire planet relies on an influx of life-affirming and life-sustaining input. In this case, the need boils down to food and species diversity.

As I had already found and would continue to find throughout my journey, humans were once again the biggest threat to an animal species. How curious that in destroying other life forms, we are absolutely endangering our own. The ocean and the plant life therein are incredibly important for the production of oxygen and the filtering of the air we must all breathe.

In addition to the trawlers, runoff from the Louros and Aracthos rivers brings with it a plethora of agricultural insecticides from farms in the area. This is contributing to the depletion of the population, as the chemicals appear to be disrupting the dolphin's reproductive cycles. It is now common for the first offspring of a female dolphin to be born malformed and unable to survive.

The female bottlenose dolphin is usually ready to reproduce at about five years of age. Before those of the Amurakikus Gulf have matured to this point, however, their bodies have been inundated with toxins that are believed to be stored in their fatty tissue. During a first pregnancy, the toxins are passed to the calf as it gestates, leading to horrific deformities that the newborns cannot survive. Subsequent pregnancies are less likely to result in malformed calves because the toxins don't have as much time to build up in the mother's body.

It is curious to see how the killing of dolphins by Japan can garner so much backlash through films like The Cove *and a number of petitions to their government, while the depletion of these animals happens worldwide. For the most part, the public is unaware of the overfishing that has led to the catastrophic decline in the dolphin population. They simply don't know how the large fisheries scoop up everything below the surface, only to pick out the fish in the highest demand and throw everything else away. Clearly, this is not a sustainable practice.*

I t was July when I arrived in Greece. I was pleased to find that, despite the heat and humidity, the weather wasn't as oppressive as I'd feared. That doesn't mean that I didn't welcome the relief afforded by the air conditioning unit in the apartment I rented at the hostel. After an afternoon out on the streets of Athens, I would open the door to the apartment and feel that cool wall of air rush forward to welcome me "home." Sometimes an audible, "Ahhhh," would escape me as my sweat-soaked shoulders greeted the sudden drop in temperature, tingling with delight.

The various hostels I stayed in all around the world played an important part in my adventure. For one thing, hostels provide some of the most affordable accommodations available. Because of this, they attract a really wide array of people, and many of them would become characters in the narrative of my journey. The people were young and old. Some were rich, and some were less-than-rich. They came from diverse backgrounds and cultures. The one thing that we all had in common, though, was our desire to be exactly where we were.

On my first evening at the Athens hostel, I visited the rooftop bar. It sat right below the Acropolis, affording an amazing view of the ancient citadel, especially when it was lit up after dark. One would expect that I'd sit there and study up on Greek history and its influence on the world, but instead, I found myself learning about the culture of Mongolia instead.

Like I said, there were all kinds of people staying at the hostel, and each had such amazing stories and insights to share. The first night, I sat with Melissa and Lisa, two twenty-something Americans. The two had been friends in high school and stayed in touch as Lisa went off to school in Missouri and Melissa joined the Peace Corps. The latter had chosen to travel with the organization to Mongolia where she'd been doing what the Peace Corps does best... helping others. The stories she shared opened my eyes to a completely different life than I was accustomed to, and the beauty of learning about it while actually living a life I wasn't accustomed to was not lost on me.

As I visited with these two reunited friends, we witnessed another reunion take place. Five young American women had been backpacking across Europe at their own paces. They had planned to meet up in Athens without coordinating via phone, each traveling in from wherever she happened to be last. Three of the group members had already arrived in Athens, and that evening the final two showed up to complete the reunion. There was much hugging and laughter, and I felt empowered by the idea that we live in a time when women can have these kinds of experiences and that they chose to have them together.

The evening continued on, bringing with it more and more new friends. The Greeks don't typically eat dinner until at least ten o'clock at night, so it was intriguing to see how the cafes began to fill up many hours after those at home would have hung out their "closed" signs. I ended up being joined for dinner by a German and a French Canadian. The former was a young lady of about 20 who was attempting to hitchhike her way across Europe. The mother in me was worried for her, but the traveler in me admired her tenacity. The latter was an Engineer, probably in his mid-twenties who was making the most of vacation time from his job.

We did our best to emulate the Greeks around us for whom this meal is an opportunity for gregarious socializing, the breaking of bread, and the leisurely enjoyment of good food. I found it to be similar to the feeling of group meals in Brazil, and had come to truly appreciate this rather un-American approach to dining. It seems to be an almost ritualized process that is in-synch with a slower, more deliberate pace of life found in so many cultures around the globe.

Speaking of "global," I continued to be introduced to folks from all over the world. After dinner, I stopped at the sports bar below my apartment for a nightcap, where I met the bartender Bob. Other patrons included an Englishman and his Scottish friend Stevie. They allowed me to join them, and we carried on for a bit before I just had to call it a night. I crawled into bed exhausted, with the sound of a dozen accents in my mind as I turned over all I had experienced in just those few hours.

The late night wasn't enough to thwart my exuberance, however, and I awoke early the next day in order to make a pilgrimage to the Acropolis before the heat could slow me down. This collection of structures lies on a rocky hill above the city, and serves as a powerful metaphor for the nation itself. There it sits, stately and impressive on top of the hill to be admired by all, just as Greece herself was once the model that other civilizations strove to emulate. And, while the Acropolis still stands, it certainly displays the marks of time. It is glorious in its own right and because of the history it represents, but it is not the shining beacon on the hill that it once was. Beautiful, but in ruins, much like the state of the country itself. From being the envy of the world to practically destitute, in no small part because of the corruption of the ideals that laid the foundation for the culture.

There was so much to see, to hear, to learn, and to simply soak in that by afternoon I was craving a nap. As I lay with my head on my pillow, I saw a vision of two men in my mind. The first was so clear that I could make out his facial features. His face was kind and gentle, his hair graying in that way many refer to as salt-and-pepper. There was nothing overly prominent about his face, there were no scars, and he was clean-shaven. The other man appeared as more of a silhouette, with a large build and wearing a button-collared shirt. After my previous experiences with "coincidences" that I no longer believed were coincidental, I took heed of what I saw; and I became pretty sure that I would meet this second man in the next couple of days, right downstairs in the sports bar.

Having gotten a bit of rest, but not quite ready to venture back out into the heat just yet, I got online to catch up on my email. I skipped past the spam and was excited to see a message from Doug, part of a father-daughter team from Boston that would be on my upcoming dolphin expedition in Vonitsa. His daughter had just graduated, and they were taking this trip together to celebrate. I opened the attached photo so I would be able to recognize them at the rendezvous point and was greeted by a man with a kind, gentle face, his hair graying in that way many refer to as salt-and-pepper.

Yep. This was the guy I saw in my vision just before I fell asleep. I was startled, of course, but happily so. For me, it was validation that I was doing a better job at listening to my intuition and recognizing the things the Universe chose to offer. It also caused me to double-down on my belief that I would be meeting the other gentleman in the bar. Listening to my gut, I was pretty sure that it wasn't going to be any sort of romantic interlude; but there seemed to be a reason that he and I were intended to meet.

Throughout the course of my trip, I had consciously chosen not to create expectations, instead allowing myself to go with the flow as opportunities made themselves known. My one exception in Greece was that I planned to experience an authentic Greek dinner with dancing that night. I was to meet Melissa and Lisa in the main lobby, but the front desk clerk informed me I had just missed them. I figured they had decided not to hang out with an "old lady" that night and chose to head out on my own, armed with directions from the clerk, Walter.

I hurried along the narrow streets, lined with homes and cafes, attempting to make it to dinner on time. Instead, I found myself turned around and unable to find my destination. I accepted that perhaps my evening plans needed to change and returned to the hostel looking a fair bit more disheveled than when I'd left 30 minutes earlier. Like everyone else in Greece, my body had a shimmer of perspiration. The humidity had left my hair in tight curls clinging to my scalp, and my throat was dry.

I was also pretty disappointed about missing out on the dining and dancing, but mustered up a positive attitude and consoled myself with the idea that everything happens for a reason. I resigned myself to grabbing a snack and a drink at the sports bar. Bob the bartender greeted me cheerfully, saying, "I am so glad you are here. I have a friend who I would like you to meet."

The friend's name was Willie, and as Bob introduced us, he mentioned that I was a psychiatric nurse and that Willie was a "nut job." I took this to be a little good-natured ribbing between buddies, but it turned out that Willie actually had some significant mental issues to deal with. While comments like Bob's are obviously not very sensitive or politically correct, they are something you come to expect in my line of work. Someone will find out my profession and immediately say things like, "Maybe I shouldn't talk to you," or "You probably have me sized up in five minutes." Some men even seem to think I must know the darkest secrets hiding in their souls.

Sure, I am fairly good at assessing people, but beyond my professional training, a lot of that can be chalked up to life skills, personal lessons, and my love of human behavior. I do have a bit of "psychic" intuition playing into it, but I certainly can't perform on command and don't have the ability to look into one's soul. Nor would I, if I could. I much prefer getting to know someone the old-fashioned way—by conversing with one another.

That said, my vision from the afternoon was right on. Willie was a hefty guy, dressed in a white, short-sleeved button down shirt. He looked to be in his fifties, with short hair that was beginning to gray a bit. He was English but had lived in Greece for most of twenty years. He'd started at the bottom, cooking his way up to a head chef position and had become quite renowned in his adopted country. At the point that I met him, though, Willie was working part-time in a low-ranking kitchen position and was actively battling his own personal demons.

The two of us sat down at a table by one of the large open windows next to the sidewalk. It was dark now, and the side street was somewhat quiet in comparison to the rest of Athens. We ordered drinks, and Willie shared a good portion of his life story with me. He grew up in a stoic, English family, headed up by an uncommunicative father who was also the police chief of their town. Feelings were never discussed in his family, despite the fact that his father likely suffered from depression. The avoidance of all things emotion-related left the home crushed by a silent, invisible fog of despair and sadness that was never acknowledged.

Willie found himself grappling with the coldness of English culture. He embraced Greece so heartily because it represented the exact opposite. The Greeks were so vagarious and family-oriented, and this was perhaps most pronounced during the evening meal. Those late dinners provided a built-in time to share and love; to eat food that leaves your palate wanting more; to drink wine, talk loudly, and laugh around the table. It was a stark contrast to Willie's upbringing.

In his younger years, Willie had studied under a chef on a private Mediterranean island owned by a Greek millionaire. During his time there, he worked his way up in the kitchen and became known and appreciated for his own style of cooking. The owner would entertain wealthy international business associates and stars from around the world. Willie spoke of preparing meals for Elizabeth Taylor and Joan Collins, and swore that Joan had tried to lure him away to be her chef in the States.

He declined the offer but did find himself growing restless. His moods began to swing, and he dove into a party lifestyle. Then, one day, he just up and went to Athens. This impulsivity became a pattern that repeated itself throughout the rest of his life. He would be invincible for a while, tirelessly working long hours, improving his skills until he was sought after by some of Greece's best restaurants. At times like this, he felt on top of the world. He would party with friends, celebrities, prostitutes, and sometimes even alone, drinking until the wee hours of the morning.

During these times, his "upswings," Willie would buy Rolex watches and Armani suits. "I loved those watches," he told me. "I couldn't get enough." He would push himself relentlessly, suffering from insomnia and not minding a bit.

Of course, these periods would be followed by times where sleeping was all he seemed able to do. Depression would lay over him like a quilt weighted down at the corners so it was impossible to throw it off. He often had suicidal thoughts and had tried to end his own life on multiple occasions by overdosing on pills. He would wake up days later feeling worse than ever and pissed off that he was still alive.

Recently, his mental and emotional difficulties had manifested in a new and dangerous symptom. Willie had developed Tourette's. He explained, "My hands and arms flail back for a moment like a convulsion while I'm working, often while I am using sharp instruments. The kitchen staff is afraid of me!" Willie was given a wide berth in the kitchen for obvious safety reasons, but the other staff were also just plain freaked out by him.

Over the years, Willie had tried a variety of anti-depressions without particularly good effects. Some helped a bit, like Prozac. "At least I had energy then and could get out of bed," he told me. When I prodded more into his medical history, he told me that he had seen many psychiatrists in both England and Greece, and had been diagnosed with depression. He went on to explain that he felt like he had tried everything from therapy to pharmaceuticals to herbal remedies. "The last doctor group I saw in England tried to help me. They asked a lot of questions like you are." He went on to tell me that they had suggested changing his meds but that he'd given in to one of those life-altering impulses that ruled him and had hooked up with some woman he didn't know and returned to Greece.

This poor man was without hope. He told me that thoughts of dying, of giving up, were with him every single day. He wanted so much to be well, but the effort was exhausting and never seemed to make the difference anyway.

While Willie's tale is a sad one, and the details of it were fairly fascinating, the basics of it were not unheard of for me. The point where my jaw dropped, however, was when he told me that when he asked his psychiatrist to take him off his current medication, due to its side effects, and to put him back on Prozac, the doctor refused. His reason, according to Willie, was because "then you will get better and leave Greece." I had heard of the rather laissez faire attitude Greeks had toward business, but I didn't realize that it extended into the medical field, too.

Then it got worse. Since the psychiatrist wouldn't treat him as he wanted, Willie would simply go to the pharmacist and tell him what to dispense. "Whaaaaat?!" I exclaimed. "You can't just write up your own prescription!" "No," he said, "but you can ask the pharmacist, and he will give it to you." My head was spinning. The entire story was amazing, and to top it off with the blatant mismanagement of his mental health was almost more than I could stand.

I asked Willie a few more psychiatric nursing assessment questions before explaining to him that while I had no authority to diagnose, his history of symptoms led me to believe it was possible that he was bi-polar. Apparently no one had ever considered this possibility with him, and he was looking to me to give him some insight. I explained that many people in that situation would go to the doctor when they were depressed and receive medication. Then, through the cycle or the disorder or due to the medication, the patient might go into a manic phase. Of course, this is the time when they feel energetic and bullet-proof, so it doesn't occur to them that this might also be a "symptom." The result is that the doctor never sees the other half of the equation in order to make the bi-polar diagnosis.

Willie and I talked for about three hours, and he was able to recognize the pattern in his behavior. I also gave him some information about mood stabilizing drugs and encouraged him to talk to his psychiatrist or pharmacist about the possibility that they might be a good option. Of course, I also explained to him the importance of being under a doctor's care if using these drugs.

It was midnight at this point, and the bar was closing. My brain was overloaded with not only my desire to help this man, but also with all of the amazing stories that had been imparted on me. I was again grateful for that earlier vision of Willie so that when I saw him, I knew there was an important reason for our meeting. I knew that I had to give him my full attention, that I needed to listen and be aware.

As we parted ways, and I made it to bed late that night, I prayed that I had given him some real hope, that perhaps he was able to look up from where he was trying to keep his head above water long enough to recognize that there was a lifeboat not too far off in the distance. I wanted desperately for him to know, to realize, to fully *understand* that there were treatment options that could manage his mood swings to find a better, happier life.

Willie said he would seriously consider returning to the doctors group in England that had been trying to help him. I pushed and pleaded, but he refused to hand over the stash of pills he kept at the ready in case today was the day he chose to end it all. He did tell me, however, that he felt very encouraged; and for someone in the depths of a bi-polar depression, even the tiniest ray of light is a significant improvement over the seemingly impenetrable blackness that holds them captive.

To this day, I have no idea if Willie followed up on my advice. I only had one more day in Athens, during which I didn't see him. From there, it was time to climb aboard the bus to Vonitsa. I think about Willie often and I so hope he found peace and happiness; and I am forever grateful for the brief time we spent together at that little table.

Throughout my travels, I looked for literature that was set in the countries I was visiting. While in Brazil, for example, I read John Grisham's *The Testament*. OK, so maybe that's not actual "literature," but much of the novel was set in the very places I was spending my time. It was an interesting study to read about my surroundings while also experiencing them through my own senses. I could look at maps in the books or read the descriptions and have them feel a bit familiar. The fact that I could read a book and have first-hand knowledge of what I would have only been visualizing otherwise was an interesting way to augment my journey and to experience both fiction and nonfiction in a whole new way.

Not too surprisingly, I found myself recognizing signs and affirmations through the books I was reading. Again, those things that might have formerly seemed like minor "coincidences" on the surface would take on a much deeper meaning and significance.

When looking for a book to take to Greece, I had hoped to find something that embodied its rich history, or even its mythology, since it has played such an important part in the development of so many different cultures. I wasn't finding anything along those lines, but as I stood in line at the second-hand store one afternoon, I noticed a book called *Dolphin Chronicles: One Woman's Quest to Understand the*

Sea's Most Mysterious Creatures. It was written by scientist Carol J. Howard who was part of a research team studying dolphins and their intelligence. Part of their project required them to capture two wild dolphins, one of each sex, within a certain age bracket. How perfect! I was going to be working with dolphins, too, so even though the book wasn't set in Greece, it seemed like a great choice.

On my way to Vonitsa to help with dolphin research myself, I cracked open the book for the first time. Within the first ten pages, there were six mentions of the fact that the author was working with the same environmental program that I was volunteering with on my endangered species expeditions. The experiences in the book took place in Miami, rather than Greece, but I certainly took it as validation of the next leg of my journey.

The book took a fascinating look at how the scientists dealt with apprehension and guilt over the fact that they were knowingly going to capture two wild animals of exceptional intelligence and then hold them in captivity for approximately two years. The author describes the onset of the mission, heading out on July 11th. I read the date again, just to make sure my brain wasn't playing a trick on me. No, the date was precisely the same as the one on the calendar that day. Though a few years apart, I was starting my dolphin expedition on the same day of the year—even the same day of the week—as the scientists in the book in my hands.

My body reacts physically to these serendipity experiences. I instantly felt so positive, so sure that I was in the right place at that moment in time. The feeling was akin to a miniature star going supernova deep within my chest.

I smiled. I probably grinned like a fool, to be honest. And there are those who might say I was. But that deep *knowing* that I was where I should be felt like a higher calling. It was a blessing and I had absolute faith in it. Others might say I have an overactive imagination or even that my brain chemistry is somehow "off," but I welcome and savor these moments when they make themselves known.

When I was making my original reservations—buying plane tickets and reserving spaces at hostels around the world—I thought I was on a quest to protect the planet's threatened animals. That was still true, of course, but such a theme developed that it was impossible for me to ignore... not that I wanted to. The overall journey had transformed from a list of tasks to accomplish into something so incredibly organic and self-sustaining. There has been little in my life that has ever empowered me the way that letting go of power has.

Dolphins represent sacredness of all life, abundance of the primordial sea. They teach us how to pass freely between this world and others. Because they are mammals, they live in 2 worlds, on top and under the sea. In doing so their mana is breath and the power of this to remind us to breath, let go, BREATH and exhale, an emotional release. Enter the water of life and then with breath and sound call forth what you most need and desire. In some cultures, because of their ability to live in 2 worlds, they are known as the messengers from a higher plane and bring messages to our dream world. It has long been believed that dolphins have superior intelligence and have long been associated in mystical lore with higher forms of consciousness. As many rescue stories have been shared about these cetaceans they are extremely protective, even of other species. Dolphins are of sea and air, caring strong intuitive and creative energy. Being highly telepathic and communicate in many ways and forms.

Still buzzing from the discoveries I'd made under the cover of the dolphin book, I arrived in the quaint village of Vonitsa late that morning. The team had plans to meet at a particular café not far from the bus station. I knew I would be the first to arrive, as Doug (the father from Boston) and I had compared itineraries. This left me with time to simply sit and stare at the water of the Amurakikus Gulf. The occasional passerby caught my eye, and I noted that no one seemed to be in a hurry. People sat at the tables of the open cafes lining the shore and took their time ordering and eating. A group of three middle-aged men huddled around a table drinking coffee and talking to each other in a way so intimate that it was clear they knew and appreciated each other deeply.

Doug and his daughter Lauren arrived right on time, bringing along a beautiful French girl named Margo. Margo was a college student and was also a part of our expedition. Next, we were joined by Joan, the Director of the dolphin expedition, and a PhD student called Giannis. Joan, the name is equivalent to John back in the states, was a striking Spaniard, probably in his early 40s and with the kind of coloring every pale white girl dreams about. Giannis was dark haired, dark eyed, and could have passed for one of the younger Greek gods. With everyone in attendance, we set off on foot to our new home for the next few days.

Unlike my previous apartment, there was no air conditioning at our new abode. Instead, we relied on strategic placement of fans to encourage at least some movement of the stagnant air. The results were tolerable. The kitchen was fairly large with a big dining table set below a window.

The view. That unassuming kitchen window afforded a view unlike any other. The rectangular opening beautifully framed the hillside of Vonitsa, showcasing the town's castle as it towered over us. It is amazing to realize that a view like that simply exists outside of a random window in someone's kitchen.

As for the kitchen itself, we were paired up in order to take turns cooking for the group. I was paired with Margo. Doug and Lauren were an obvious matchup, and Joan and Giannis were the third team. A Greek, a Franc, a Spaniard, and three Americans walk into a bar...It doesn't have quite the same punch as the jokes along those lines, but it was real life. The meals we shared at that table, laughing as the castle stood guard through the window, were some of the most fun, educational, and thought provoking times of my life. We would eat early by Greek standards—maybe 9 p.m.—enjoying our victuals and a bottle of wine before turning in to be ready for our 6 a.m. wakeup call.

The group of us were on the boat by seven, yawning in the sea air as the vessel glided through the glass-like water. We could see well into the distance and kept our eyes on the surface in hopes of sighting dolphins. It was essential for us to travel the water by way of a very specific grid pattern to ensure that our research was as consistent and accurate as possible. Each team member was responsible for an area of water, keeping an intent watch on our section in search of dolphins.

The pattern was based on the face of a clock. The bow

of the boat represented twelve o'clock, and the person positioned there was responsible for scanning the water from twelve to three. The starboard person monitored the area representing three to six, and so on. When one of the volunteers or researchers spotted a dolphin, we would yell out the sighting in the format of number of dolphins, activity, position, and distance from the boat. For example, if we saw two dolphins leaping and splashing off the starboard side, the person responsible for that part of the grid would yell, "Two. Ariel. At three o'clock. One hundred meters."

The graduate student Giannis would then log the information, and Joan would photograph the animals' fins. Later on the volunteers would be able to identify the fins, and the data would be added to a computerized system. Fins are actually a wonderful identifier for dolphins. Each can be as unique as a fingerprint, and their appearance is a peek into the animal's personal history and life experiences.

For example, dolphins like to play rough. They jump and dive, but they also chase each other, slipping through the water silently, or chirping away delightedly. This play can lead to injuries or marks on their fins. They also tend to show aggression by "raking," which is scratching one another with their teeth. This can leave behind superficial lacerations that heal up but leave behind scars. The result is traces of lighter strips running parallel to one another on the dolphin's skin. A rather adorable means for them to show aggression, by the way, is to emit bubble clouds from their blowholes. Because, what is more intimidating than bubbles, right?

Fins can also be marked up as a result of the terrain where the dolphin lives and swims, not to mention from interactions with predators. Some fins have scrapes while others are missing entire chunks along the edges. Because of these unique markings, it is often fairly easy for researchers to identify a particular animal with little more than a glance. The underlying motivation for the searching was to locate a small group, which we referred to as the "home group." Our job was to collect a variety of data about this group, such as the number of animals, each one's size and age, and their behaviors. This would be compiled with photos of their fins for identification and added to the growing body of data about the home group and its habits.

At times we would come across small groups of dolphins, but other times we would encounter much larger pods. Typically, dolphins swim in groups of two to fifteen, even forming social bonds with the members of their group. Sticking with any particular home group can be tricky, as dolphins are fast swimmers and can submerge under water for up to eight minutes at a time. So it became a game of hide-and-go-seek where the researchers were always "it."

In order for the data to be consistent and usable, there were some fairly stringent guidelines in place. For example, if new members joined a home group, or an original member left, the group had to be omitted from study. The reasoning for this was that the change of dynamics among the home group's members would affect their behavior, making the data inaccurate.

There's no doubt that humans feel drawn to dolphins. They are naturally lovable, with their round, almost chubby features and playful nature. In ways, I think they remind us of human toddlers, something our brains have been hardwired to adore and protect for the survival of our own species. One of the behaviors the dolphins engaged in was "scouting" by swimming alongside the boat and then leaping out of the water far enough to see what was happening on board. When this happened, the animals would actually make eye contact with you, making you wonder just how much of the situation they grasped in their fairly advanced brains. I could almost swear that one dolphin in particular winked at me!

Another of their more famous behaviors is that of "bow riding." As a boat pushes its way through the water, it creates an undercurrent radiating out from around the bow and the stern. We often think of the "wake" of the boat coming off the back, but the front also has to cut through the sea water, channeling it along either side of the vessel. The dolphins find this quite entertaining and will basically surf the waves created, albeit they are underwater as opposed to a surfer who uses a board on the surface. It is thought that riding the bow waves or stern wake might be adapted from the natural behavior of riding ocean swells or even traveling in the wakes of large whales. Baby dolphins travel in their mother's side stream, or hydrodynamic wake, too.

The energetic activity of leaping and splashing that dolphins are so well known for is called "breaching." Dolphins can jump as high as 4.9 meters (16 feet) from the surface of the water, and will land on their backs, bellies, or sides. It's almost impossible not to giggle and smile when they're engaging in this behavior, because they are clearly having so much fun.

Also impressive are the "aerials" that the dolphins often perform. They will spring from the ocean's surface with enough velocity to propel their entire bodies upward in order to execute spins and other aerodynamics that would make a gymnast jealous, all before landing nose-first in the water.

There are some less famous dolphin behaviors, which are still quite fascinating. For example "percussion" refers to a type of movement in which the dolphin extends all of its body from the water with the exception of its tail before slapping its body down. They can also "stand" on their tails, propelling the body out of the water and skimming forward in this manner. Dolphins swim erratically, switching direction in the blink of an eye.

While it's impossible to know for certain all of the biological implications of these behaviors, there are some well-educated guesses. Many of them are thought to be done in "play." Throughout the animal kingdom, playing isn't just about having a good time, it's also about learning survival skills. That's why when you see baby predators playing, they're usually slinking, pouncing, and attacking. On the other hand, animals more likely to grow up to be prey engage in play that is more about running and jumping—in other words, evasive maneuvers. In addition to dolphins playing in this manner, it's also thought that some of the behaviors are related to both socializing and attracting food.

Our first full day out was fairly successful. We scanned the water for quite some time before finally catching sight of the object of our study. We found a group that we could focus on to collect data. Joan barked out orders like a pirate, gruff and without mincing words and wasting precious time.

I've often referred to the overall experience of globe hopping as a "quest," a "journey," or "my travels." At the point where Joan was shouting orders as the boat whizzed through the water on the trail of a home group of bottlenose dolphins in the Amurukikus Gulf, the word that I would have chosen was "adventure." There was no doubt that I was truly on an adventure.

It was hard to believe that Joan lived this life every day. What was an unbelievable adventure to me was simply waking up in the morning and going to work for him. Joan had a rogue sort of style to him, but it was tempered with a dash of a romanticism—whether his nature or my own ideas projected onto him, I'm not completely sure. He told me he could never marry due to the research and how much travel it involved. It could be hard to see why someone would forego a "normal" life to dedicate every waking moment to a group of animals that couldn't care less one way or another if you counted how many times they slapped their tail on the surface of the water or took pictures of their fins. The next day, however, I was offered some amazing insight into what drove Joan and the others to keep at their thankless work.

The air was hot, even at eight a.m., and the breeze created by moving across the ocean's surface wasn't enough to combat the temperature. I noticed that the sea air on the gulf didn't taste of salt like I remembered from my days of living on the beach in Southern California. The air here seemed much heavier. We were soon distracted from the atmospheric conditions, however, as we neared a group of dolphins. Each team member had his or her turn at yelling out research data from their designated position in the boat.

"Four. Aerial. Three o'clock. At 60 meters!"

"Two. Breaching. Twelve o'clock. At 45 meters!"

"Four. Percussion. Nine o'clock. At 25 meters!"

There were so many sightings that we all ended up yelling information simultaneously, flooding Joan and Giannis with data faster than they could record it. Our own excitement was growing, and we were hollering, grinning, and trying to keep up with what we saw in our part of the grid.

After a few rounds of this, Joan bellowed, "STOP!"

The boat slowed to a drift. In succession, each of us grasped what was happening. Our eyes and smiles grew wide. As we looked out onto the water, allowing ourselves to take it all in, we realized that we were absolutely surrounded by dolphins. There were as many as 100 of them bobbing and diving, their wet skin smooth and shining under the Greek sun.

Joan and Giannis were laughing with unabashed joy, hooting and cheering, unable to believe their eyes. Anywhere you looked to five hundred meters out, dolphins were breaching, splashing, and doing aerials. They leapt, frolicked, and rode the current created by the boat. "This never happens!" our awe-struck leaders told us again and again.

As I smiled to myself amidst the spectacle, I thought, "Oh, yes it does! Thank you, Universe, for this gift!" Joan and Giannis spent their careers studying these animals, and yet they had never seen such a display. Somehow, I happened to be standing on the deck of a boat in the Mediterranean Sea when it happened. Those few minutes spent observing the beauty, grace, and wild abandon of the dolphins were some of the most joyful of my entire life. As had happened so many times during my journey, I felt my existence and comprehension of the world expand within me. Something that was completely outside the realm of belief five minutes ago had come crashing...splashing...into existence.

The rest of the week definitely had its highs and lows. We saw a good number of home groups and gathered data on them, which was very satisfying. On the other end of the emotional spectrum, however, we witnessed first-hand the tragic effects of agricultural pollution. For the first five years or so of a female bottlenose dolphin's life, her body tries to deal with the toxic insecticides flushed into the sea by the Louros and Aracthos rivers by storing them in her fatty tissues, thereby keeping the dangerous chemicals from moving into her vital organs or otherwise killing her.

During pregnancy, these toxins are transferred to the fetus, causing horrendous and fatal birth defects. On our data-gathering mission one day, we came across a small calf with a malformed, bulbous head. The baby was struggling to even swim. There was a small group of dolphins, including his mother, that would try to encourage it, but the calf simply couldn't keep up. The group would move on, and the mother and baby would lag behind until another group joined up with them. We learned that the calf would probably only survive another day or two. It was a heartbreaking revelation, compounded by the fact that in such an intelligent species, the calf's death would likely be especially hard for the mother.

With the danger from pollution, the lack of diversity of food, and extreme overfishing by the fisheries— who seem to have little to no oversight— the dolphins of the Amurakikus Gulf are facing a dire situation, indeed. Many of the local, smaller fishermen are actively trying to reverse the trend by employing sustainable fishing practices. Unfortunately, the larger fisheries are more concerned with grabbing up the high-demand fish to sell for top dollar, and they scoop up everything else along the way.

Sustainable fishing needs to be a priority, not just in the

Mediterranean, but worldwide. The problem of dead spots in the ocean and its increasing inability to function as a source of oxygen and filtration system for the air is one that has dire global implications. While our focus was obviously on understanding and protecting the dolphin population, the problem extends so much further, touching every single life on the planet. We, as consumers, can have a direct and dramatic impact on sustainable fishing practices through our buying choices. By asking the simple question, "Was this fish caught sustainably?" we can make a statement to those providing the food. Trawling is not sustainable. Fish farms are not sustainable. Fish should be wild-caught in limited numbers.

On a more positive note, there were many wonderful experiences throughout the rest of the expedition, both on the boat and off. We would leave the docks at about seven each morning, and around ten we would dock in a different village. This was a wonderful way to experience Greek culture outside of the big city of Athens. These breaks usually included good coffee and snacking on the local specialty before heading back out to sea for a couple more hours of dolphin sighting.

Most afternoons we would dock back in Vonitsa and have a quick beverage at Joan's favorite family-owned café while discussing plans for the rest of the day. To be honest, our plans usually looked about the same: We would have lunch, take a two-hour siesta until four o'clock, and then pair up to review the photos taken and identify the individual dolphins. Early evenings were devoted to a lecture or documentary to further our knowledge of dolphins and the environment.

Dinner was served around 9 p.m., and if I wasn't on kitchen duty, I would enjoy some down-time before everyone gathered around the table to partake. During this time, Giannis would expound on his feelings about Greek politics and how they related to the culture. His feelings were echoed by many of the Greeks I met who all seemed to feel that, even if change were possible, it would be a long time coming. They would tell me with resigned sighs about levels of corruption that make the American political system look positively saintly, and would often follow it up with comments like, "It is what it is. It is our culture."

The country is so old, and the ways are very, very ingrained. Like the raping of the sea floor by the trawlers, the ill effects of greed and disregard can be seen all over Greece. Despite a floundering economy and outright anger, however, the Greeks are still very proud people. And they should be. An incredible amount of what modern Westerners take for granted is rooted in Greek culture. The influence on art, drama, and literature, for example, is profound. From the English language to the foundations of medicine to basic philosophical understandings, so much of the present was informed by the Greece of the past.

Greece used to be the leader of the "civilized" world. It was the patriarch of the Western nations that would follow. But, just as Great Grandpa isn't quite the same man you see when you sift through those old black-and-white photos of him in his WWII uniform, Greece has also grown frailer and perhaps a little eccentric. You can offer your respect and admiration for what has been, but sometimes you want to shake your head and say, "Grandpa! That's not how we do things anymore!" Of course, he doesn't care all that much, preferring to enjoy his beautiful retirement on the Mediterranean.

Like the country hosting me, I had been changed through loss. I was also struggling to reconcile my past with my present. I was no longer a wife, for example. While it may have appeared that I was off on a whirl-wind vacation and didn't give a second thought to the marriage behind me, that was certainly not the case. I felt the pain of that loss acutely, and I found it surfacing like that poor baby dolphin. The marriage had started with such joy and potential, and there had been much love and affection for as long as possible, but in the end, it lacked the strength needed to continue rising to the surface for air and sank while those who were invested in it grieved.

At times, I would think I had dealt with my divorce or with the loss of my stepfather, but then I would find myself in some far-flung country dealing with a whole new layer of pain. Each of those layers was different, and each had to be uncovered and worked through. Little reminders would unexpectedly kick up a thought about the past, and there would be fresh tears. Sometimes they would be tears of grief. Sometimes they were a result of an onset of loneliness. Sometimes they carried my fears for the future. The tears were different, just as the layers were different, and it seemed I had to go through them all.

Greece has experienced economic disaster and is no longer the shining example for the world, but that will never erase its illustrious history and influence on so much of civilization. That will exist from now until the end of the earth. The people there are proud of where they come from, not just geographically, but also historically. Sometimes they mourn for what has been lost, and sometimes they are discontent with where they are, but they revel in life and focus on what makes them joyful. I would do the same, I thought, as I left Greece behind and embarked on the most anticipated part of my quest.

A photo opportunity while out measuring Acacia trees.

Ol Pejeta Conservancy, Kenya

View from our jeep

Ol Pejeta Conservancy, Kenya

1 month after EF5 tornado

Joplin, Missouri

View from my campsite

Mount Kenya, Ol Pejeta Conservancy, Kenya

Castle over looking the town.

Vonitsa, Greece

Up close and personal while sitting in jeep.

Ol Pejeta Conservancy, Kenya

Strolled right on by while we were in the jeep.

Ol Pejeta Conservancy, Kenya

At Drs Silveira and Jacomo's animal refuge at their home.

Emos National Forest, Brazil

View from water's vantage.

Igauzu Falls, Argentina side, Brazil

Sweetwater Chimpanzee Sanctuary

Ol Pejeta, Kenya

CHAPTER 6

Kenya

The black rhino is nearly extinct. In Kenya, the number of these animals dropped from 20,000 in 1970 to 539 in 2012. There are approximately 150 zoos in North America and Europe, and when the animals in captivity are included, the world population for the black rhino is estimated to be about 2,500.

Without a doubt, the biggest threat to the black rhino is humankind. They have no real predators, although a pride of lionesses may occasionally try for one if other food sources are scarce. Instead, these animals have been hunted almost to extinction for their horns. Made not of bone, the horn is actually comprised of a skin-like material. All kinds of magical properties have been attributed to the rhino's horn, and *unscrupulous hunters are willing to wipe out the entire population in order to poach this one part of the animal to sell on the black market.*

In a spiritual sense, the rhinoceros represents ancient wisdom. The name comes from two words. "Rhino," meaning "nose," and "keras," meaning "horn." They are solitary animals and descended from ancient times, bringing with them a special kind of energy that seems to make them quite comfortable in solitude.

Unlike other horned animals, the rhino's horn is located on the nose, rather than the top of the head. This results in greater olfactory awareness. The sense of smell has long been a symbol of higher discrimination, spiritual idealism, and the application of higher wisdom. These animals also have a keen sense of hearing, although their eyesight is poor.

When you put these ideas together, the rhinoceros becomes a physical embodiment of trusting one's own inner wisdom. The rhino doesn't subscribe to the herd mentality and pays close attention to its most developed senses. If something doesn't smell right, they follow their inner wisdom. If only we humans could do the same.

The plane eventually arrived in Nairobi in the wee hours of the morning on July 23rd. By the time I got through customs and collected my luggage, it was five a.m. It was still dark when I went outside to hail a taxi, and the cool air was refreshing as it caressed my travel-worn body. I had spent so many hours cooped up in airports and planes over the previous two days and was relieved to be in a part of the world where the temperatures would drop at night.

I was dressed in a short-sleeved shirt and cargo pants, an obvious contrast to the cab drivers and parking attendants who were all bundled up in hooded parkas for this chilly 50 degree weather. As I walked to my taxi, I was awed by the fact that I was breathing African air! The driver welcomed me with a bright smile, his dazzling white teeth so stark against his dark, dark skin. Throughout my time in Africa, I would be greeted warmly, but it was especially sweet in Kenya where the lovely accent made for a melodic greeting as they sincerely bid, *"Jambo!* Welcome to Kenya!" Each time, it felt like a loving embrace.

For the most part, the Kenyans I met were very poor and quite humble, but as I traveled across the country, I came to learn how proud they were that the US president had Kenyan bloodlines. While Barack Obama may not have been raised in their country, they still felt a sense of pride at sharing his heritage. All throughout my travels, and especially in Kenya, I was told how lucky I was to be a natural born citizen of the United States. The wealth and freedoms that US Americans have available is an impossible dream for the vast majority of those on the African continent.

In fact, an urban ghetto in the United States would be a welcome experience for many Kenyans living in abject poverty. When I later returned to my safe, cozy neighborhood in the Pacific Northwest, I would often find myself walking along safely, recalling so many of the people I had met who were denied that privilege. I tried to imagine the extent of the awe they would feel if they were there, walking alongside me.

One of the things often overlooked when it comes to experiencing and learning about another culture is how much it can bring your own culture into focus. Things we often take for granted or even consider "human nature" are actually a product of our cultural and societal upbringings. Experiencing the extreme poverty of Kenya brought me a deeper appreciation of our country's wealth. We have miles and miles of towns and cities, all filled with houses and businesses. Even our "low-income" neighborhoods would be considered luxurious by many of these people's standards. And my middle-class neighborhood? Those I met in Kenya would likely have thought they'd arrived in Oz via hot air balloon.

The neighborhoods I saw in Kenya were miles deep, as well, but there was little resemblance to anything I was used to. Homes were constructed from whatever materials could be salvaged: metal sheets, cardboard, and—if you were lucky enough to find any—maybe some lumber scraps. These pieces of cast-off material, things that others felt were only worth being discarded, made up the walls and ceilings of entire families' homes. There were no windows to speak of, and in place of doors were either gaping entranceways or sheets of fabric strung up to afford some small bit of privacy to the inhabitants.

And, yet, these people were grateful for what they had. There was no wall-to-wall carpeting; rather the shanties were built directly upon the dirt, with the earth acting as the floor. Those living within the scavenged walls were thankful for that dirt beneath their feet. Without it, they would have nothing.

Nairobi was a bustling city, unlike anything I had ever experienced before. The types of safety regulations that surround transportation in the US were clearly not a high priority in the cities of Kenya. Volkswagen-type vans were filled with twelve or more passengers packed intimately close to one another while an attendant stood in the open door space. The entire group moved as one while the vehicle maneuvered in and out of traffic, one of thousands of mini-buses just like it.

Motorcycles carried two and three passengers at a time, of course without helmets. They could zip through small gaps in the labyrinth of traffic, weaving back and forth, speeding, slowing, stopping when necessary. The movements in the streets and sidewalks seemed to be endless. Despite my fair skin and curly strawberry blond hair, I never felt out of place in that throng of humanity, pushing along like blood pumped through the city's veins. The culture is very polite and reserved, and as a result, I never noticed anyone staring at me. Never was a degrading remark directed at me. I simply joined the flow like everyone else.

My hotel, The Fairview, was beautiful. It sat atop a hill in the center of Nairobi, so the name was quite fitting, as the view was stunning. Once inside the grounds of The Fairview, it was nearly impossible to believe that such a large, busy city sat just beyond the gates. Guests were instead treated to lush tropical gardens, waterfalls, and a variety of cafes and eateries. Talented musicians strummed and sang as they strolled the property, filling the grounds with an array of sights and sounds that delighted my senses. The food and service were superb, with the staff and other guests being exceptionally kind.

Not only was this grand hotel fit for royalty, but so was its security. This wasn't apparent with just a glance, however. The unarmed guards who stood at the entrance and were scattered about the grounds seemed unthreatening. Each was friendly and polite. What made it so secure was the fact that it was located across the street from the Israeli Embassy. Because of the proximity, hotel guests drove through a near obstacle course of cement cylinders and submitted to security checks. Armed guards questioned drivers and passengers about their business status, automobiles were searched thoroughly—inside, outside, under the luggage on the roof—and the entire street was lined with more armed guards in uniform. It was intense, to say the least.

From time to time, an agent of the Embassy would circulate the hotel grounds. Neither before nor after in my life have I ever seen a human being who radiated such earnestness. I wondered if he ever smiled in his private life, because that obviously wasn't something he did during work hours. Did he experience frequent headaches, or did he find moments to relax and breathe deeply? The Israeli Embassy had been bombed in 1998, which explained the extensive security. In fact, it's likely that some of the hotel staff were also Embassy agents working under cover. I was more than likely staying at the safest hotel in all of Kenya.

On the morning of the 25th, the entire volunteer black rhino research team met up in the parking lot of The Fairview. There were twelve members, including myself, all of whom were from the US. When I found this out, I felt a little deflated. So much of my journey up to that point had been impacted by the addition of volunteers from other countries, and I had been looking forward to adding to my growing list of culture trivia. For example, the Belgian Constitution guarantees the "freedom of language," protecting citizens' right to speak any language they choose in the private sphere. In Brazil, eye contact during conversation is common and sustained. Germany's Oktoberfest actually begins on a

Saturday in September (but not always the same one). These are the kinds of small but fascinating tidbits one picks up from spending time with volunteers from other countries, and I was sorry I would be missing out on that during this leg of the trip.

The Americans in our group, however, did represent many geographical regions. Members hailed from the West Coast, the Northwest, the South, the Midwest, and along the East Coast. We ranged in age from 18 to 72. Our transportation was not luxurious by any means. We all squeezed into a minivan with our driver, our entire bounty of luggage secured to the top of the van or tucked under our seats.

Our destination that day was the Ol Pejeta Conservancy. We passed through towns and countryside, and my consciousness continued to expand as my awareness of the world did likewise. We drove by locals walking to and from the market, some balancing all manner of items on their heads. Children herded goats. A bicyclist carried an impossibly large bundle of sticks for fencing. Others used their bikes to transport bundles of plantains to sell at the market, pushing their bicycles up and down the mountain roads when necessary. And always, the waving children on the roadside with their enthusiastic smiles.

Soon after we entered the Conservancy, a giraffe came into view. As we looked closer, we saw that the tall animal was following behind a lioness. "Is this a Disney movie?" I asked my fellow passengers. That image—a giraffe casually following a lion through an open green field—seemed like it could only happen in a cartoon. If I had imagined the scene, surely the lioness would have been stalking and pouncing on the giraffe.

Our driver brought the van to a stop on the roadside to allow us to take in the sight. With no hint of fear, the lioness strolled over to the road and sat right next to the van. She posed patiently as we all madly clicked away with our cameras. The remainder of the drive to camp continued to unfold wonders. We observed elephants, a great kudus, warthogs, impalas, and zebras.

At the camp, we met two paleontologists for the Smithsonian museum. Both had done their PhD dissertation research at Ol Pejeta and were now engaging in a few weeks' worth of continued research. The two women were surprised when we recounted our many sightings during the drive. "That is amazing!" they informed us. "We never see that many animals in such a short time span!" The volunteers all looked at each other in confusion. We just assumed that what we were seeing was part of the typical day in Africa. When the scientist went on to explain that there are often only one or two sightings a day, I tipped my hat to the Universe and accepted this gift to start my next adventure.

We each settled into our separate huts, which were six-foot mud brick walls and thatched roofs comprising a round room, approximately twenty feet in diameter. Wild critters have been known to find their way into the huts, despite the reinforcements. Our new paleontologist friends shared stories of their surprise encounters, and we quickly learned to pause before entering once we'd opened a door. That allowed a moment for us to determine if a snake would fall from the top of the door and to listen for the scurry of paws running across the floor.

The huts themselves encircled the main entrance of the camp. In the center was a semi-landscaped lawn area of sorts, with a variety of bushes and a sign that read "Beware of Wild Animals." This was a friendly reminder that even though you might feel like you were at a quaint outdoor retreat, you should not let your guard down. This fact was driven home the first day as a group of baboons ran across the grounds, hooting and tumbling, as they made their way past that very sign.

The baboons were large and intimidating. Each weighed between 30 and 80 pounds and was 2 to 4 feet tall. In spite the sinewy strength of muscles that are built for hurling an animal from branch to branch, it is perhaps the fangs that are most frightening. This was definitely not a petting zoo.

We were also reminded to be careful at night if needing to use the bathroom facilities. Apparently hippos from a nearby lake would occasionally wander in to graze during the night. "Um...don't they stay in the water?" I questioned anxiously. After-dark hippo parades in front of the bathrooms was definitely not something I remembered ever seeing mentioned on any of the nature shows I'd watched. This warning bolstered my plan of making sure my bladder was good and empty before going to bed each night. I'd originally been worried about lions and hyenas out roaming during the night, and now it seemed I could add hippos to that list of potential hazards.

No, thanks. I thought. *I am not walking next door to use the toilet, only to get the pee scared out of me on the way there. That would defeat my original purpose and probably end with me being stomped by a four-ton hippo!*

During my time at the camp, I would drift off at night, tucked in to bed and listening to the hyenas talk and howl to one another. Just before dawn, I would be awakened by a sound that made me think some of the staff members were crazy enough to keep little yappy dogs out in the wilds of Kenya. I was confused as to how they could be so callous as to let the little doggies out every morning, their yelps basically advertising them as a breakfast appetizer. It was a few days before I discovered that the strange sound was actually a herd of zebras. It was shocking to think I had been looking at pictures of zebras throughout my entire life without the vaguest idea of what they sounded like.

Roused from sleep by the zebras, we volunteers were ready to leave camp by seven a.m. each day. Preparations included recalibrating our GPS tracking devices for the day, gathering tools, loading backpacks, and eating breakfast. This also happened to be the best time of day for viewing Mt. Kenya, as by nine a.m., the clouds closed in around its peak. But, first thing in the morning, the view was unobscured, and the magnificence of the landform was undeniable. Each morning, as I stepped out of my hut, this majestic landform welcomed me to a new day in Kenya, and I was filled with wonder each and every time.

When I arrived at Ol Pejeta Conservancy, there were 79 black rhinos. A week before, there had been 80. For the first time in two years, a poacher had taken a rhino. Despite strict security, both on land and in the air, the poacher had succeeded in taking one of the animals down. In turn, the hunter was killed in the ensuing raid. It was a grim reminder of how determined humans can be to destroy something simply for financial gain, and a testament to how dedicated others are to protecting the few rhinos that remain.

Our job was not just simply to keep track of the black rhino, but more importantly to monitor their food supply. Ninety-nine percent of a black rhino's food comes from the acacia tree. In one of those amazing quirks of nature, it turned out that a 3,000 pound animal with skin like armor and a presence that intimidates pretty much every other living animal, survives almost exclusively off of a thorny, scrawny looking tree with skinny little leaves.

Our task, day after day, was to work with a partner to measure the trees. I was paired up with a retired teacher named Kathy. She was the oldest member of our group, but due to her vitality and personality, she was one of those people you would use the modifier "years young" to describe. As in, "Kathy was 72 years young." This was not some decrepit schoolmarm; rather, she was a passionate member of the team.

There were acres of acacia trees for us to survey. From the tiniest seedling to the largest mature tree, we measured height, diameter, and longest limb, as well as making notes about any particular damage to the tree. For example, some trees may have been knocked down by elephants, rhinos or giraffes could have nibbled away at the leaves, or natural causes like drought or fire could have inflicted damage. We were charged with recording all of this. Some lots included numbered trees that had been monitored for as many as ten years. Each had a detailed history to which we would add our notes.

This sounds like an easy enough task, but it was actually quite complicated. We used GPS tracking information from past volunteers, but with weather, the passage of time, and a little room for error, it often felt like embarking on a treasure hunt. These trees are crucial in the survival of the rhino, so the work is important in their conservation.

The trees were also in peril. Elephants are known to destroy large areas of the acacia as they barrel through, knocking down whatever is in their path, or even breaking the trees in half on purpose. There is a variety of ants that like to house themselves in the acacia. When the elephant attempts to eat the tree, the little buggers crawl up their nostrils. The elephants get around this by ripping the tree apart and lying the branches on the ground for a while to encourage the ants to scurry away. The elephant comes back later for a less bothersome meal. It's a very clever strategy, but it isn't such a great thing for the trees.

Other animals pose problems, too. Both giraffes and baboons enjoy munching on the new blossoms of the acacia tree. When these are nipped off, however, it keeps the plant from going to seed. The result, of course, is fewer saplings to continue the cycle of life.

One cool morning, as we prepared to head out to our various sites, the group split up into two jeeps. I was in the lead jeep, busily discussing plans for the day with the Director, Dr. Geoffrey Wahungu, when he pointed ahead and called, "Slow down! Look!" Approximately ten meters up the dirt road, a couple of wild dogs appeared from the bushes that lined the roadside. They trotted into the middle of the road and sat down as if they were waiting for us. More dogs made their way out of the bushes, joining the others, tilting their heads and sizing us up. From the jeep, we likely mirrored them, tilting our own heads and peering at the incredible sight.

Two of the dogs, one of which was possibly the leader of the pack, broke from the others. His coat was a beautiful tortoiseshell pattern from the top of his round ears to the tip of his wagging tail. His buddy was almost completely black. The two bold fellows sniffed at the jeep, while those of us inside held our breath. There was a bit of fear, but mostly, we just didn't want to scare the wild dogs away. It worked, and the rest of the pack, maybe eight more animals, followed suit, although they kept a little more distance and fanned out.

We volunteers were certainly awed by the experience, but it turned out that we weren't the only ones. According to Geoffrey, in his ten-plus years in the area, that was his first sighting of wild dogs. One of the guards, Solomon, chimed in to tell us that this was only his second sighting in seventeen years. Considering the jaguar in Brazil, the dolphins in Greece, and so many of the other experiences I'd had in my travels, I was starting to get comfortable with these "rare" sightings!

I hadn't realized that the wild dogs were also threatened, fighting for a place to exist on this planet. That night, I laid in my bunk and cried. I cried for the beauty of the animals and the opportunity we were given to see them in their full glory like that. I cried over how they seemed to almost be watching over us, when in reality people are probably their worst enemy. I cried at the continued gifts from the Universe and for the fact that Africa felt so real and raw and beautiful and sad and blessed and forsaken. So many contradictions co-existed in the same amazing place.

The black rhino is certainly not the only endangered animal in Kenya. Some others include cheetahs, chimpanzees, Jackson hartebeests, Grevy's zebras, and silverback gorillas; and we volunteers were able to experience some of these species, too. There were 20 cheetahs at the Ol Pejeta Conservancy, and I was fortunate enough to see some up close. In fact, one sauntered in front of our parked jeep. I was riding shotgun and watched in awe as the big cat strutted its way towards us across the grasslands, against a backdrop of low-lying mountains that ensured the scene was picture perfect.

I was captivated by its elegance and grace. It walked the wilds like a sleek haute couture model walks the runways of Milan. As it moved along without a hint of self-consciousness, its spots appeared to separate from its fur, creating a three-dimensional illusion that made it clear how it camouflaged itself among the sun and shadows. I had never expected to fall so hard and so fast for the cheetah, but it immediately made its way onto my list, coming in a close second to the jaguar as my favorite animal.

Perhaps it's my freckled skin and petite frame that make me feel so aligned with these spotted cats. I just find everything about them to be so alluring, right down to the intensity of their mere presence. Both the cheetah and the jaguar are loners, relying on themselves—on their own stealth, strength, and agility—as they interact with the world around them.

Part of the program in Kenya included various outings. One of these was to the Sweetwater Chimpanzee Sanctuary. Until my travels, I had been unaware that chimpanzees were a threatened species. Though not native to this area, this particular sanctuary was established in 1993 by Jane Goodall to receive and provide refuge to chimpanzees that had been orphaned or abused.

There were 42 chimps at Sweetwater, living in two large groups separated by the Ewasu Nyiro River. Chimpanzees are territorial and will fight to the death, so it is necessary to keep the groups separated. The Chimpanzee is the closest living relative to humans, sharing approximately 98% of our genetic blueprint.

The stories we heard about the abuse and neglect endured by the animals residing at the sanctuary was heartbreaking. While I was somewhat prepared for tales of chimps abused in captivity, one big surprise was the existence of the "bush meat" market. In densely forested areas, it is nearly impossible to farm, and it can be a struggle for human families to survive. From generation to generation, the solution handed down has been to buy bush meat. Bush meat is any type of animal that comes from the jungle, with the most popular being the chimpanzee.

It is estimated that nearly 12,000 pounds of bush meat is smuggled into other parts of Africa, as well as France, every single week. As the animals' habitat is destroyed by logging, another danger is introduced in the form of better access for poachers. Adult chimps are killed for commercial bush meat without any regard for orphaned infants left behind, unless it is to capture them to be sold as exotic pets. Only about 25% of these captured infants survive.

The story of the Grevy's zebra's struggle with extinction is a little different, but no less distressing. Farms and ranches have encroached on the zebras' habitat, bringing with them livestock and competition for food. Not only is there less grazing area available, but access to water has also been greatly reduced due to fencing and agricultural irrigation. To make matters worse, the Grevy's zebra is also hunted for its meat and skin, and parts of the animal are used in traditional medicines. Such big changes in the habitat have left the zebras susceptible to new diseases and parasites. In 2005, more than 50 Grevy's zebras in Kenya died from an outbreak of anthrax.

These zebras have undergone one of the most substantial redirections of range of any African mammal. Confined to the Horn of Africa, Ethiopia, and Kenya, the global population at the end of the 1970s was approximately 15,000. By 2008, that number dipped to a distressing 2,500. This is more than an 80% decline in global numbers over the course of only three decades! That means that the death of those 50 zebras due to anthrax wiped out about two percent of the population. For perspective, if something that catastrophic happened to the human population, it would kill about 141 million people.

Interestingly, the Grevy's zebra took its survival into its own hands with some strategies for adaptation. For example, the more common zebra, with its slightly smaller stature and wider stripes, doesn't seem to suffer from the same perils as its cousin. Perhaps through some instinctual, evolutionary urge to pass on their genes, or just not enough hot female Grevy'ss around, some males started breeding with common zebra females. The product is a medium-sized, striped zebra.

This was seen at the Ol Pejeta Conservancy, where there were eight Grevy's residing alongside thousands of common zebras. When the Grevy's population didn't rise, the scientists found that the Grevy's males had been mating with the common females. Some of the offspring from these unions were sterile, such as is the case with mules and hinnies that result from the union of a donkey and a horse. Because of this, the Conservancy transported in eight more Grevy's to shake things up a bit. Throw in a full moon and some violin music, and the tone should be just right for a little zebra romance.

All joking aside, however, these animals are not only beautiful, but they are also part of the balance of nature in Kenya. To lose them would be an absolute tragedy.

Toward the end of our first week at the Conservancy, Kathy and I got a turn to go on the wildlife scout. Joining us were Hailey, her work partner Bill, and our guard Solomon. Any time we went out in the field, we were accompanied by an armed guard. In the ten-year history of Earthwatch in this area, there had never been an incident more serious than firing off a couple of rifle rounds to scare away a lion. This was comforting, as when we were out taking stock of the acacia trees, there would often be groups of warthogs watching from the perimeter—typically in groups of three. Before venturing to the wilds of Africa, one of my biggest fears was being attacked by a wild boar. When I arrived at the Conservancy and saw that there were thousands of these beasts all around, I worried that I'd never be able to step foot outside of the jeep.

But with the assurance of the guards, I was able to find that, although warthogs can certainly be dangerous, they're also quiet charming and endearing. They have a curious nature and a face that only a mother could love. They would trot along busily with their tails pointing straight up, just like in *The Lion King*. I became so amused by them that I couldn't help but giggle whenever they came by to check us out.

Our small group was dropped off at a location that had not yet been monitored on this expedition. Kathy and I would be keeping track of the wildlife: taking note of the variety of animals, their sexes, number of offspring, etc. and entering the data into our GPS systems. Hailey and Bill had the oh-so-glamorous job of counting elephant dung. Some people just have all the luck! Counting the dung actually serves an important purpose by tracking where the elephants are and their numbers in order to anticipate the type of damage that they will do to the habitat. Information regarding the amount, freshness, and other factors was recorded.

The very moment we stepped out of the jeep that morning, an uneasy feeling settled within me. The five of us trekked off into the fields and bushes. We kept as quiet as possible to avoid interrupting the daily goings on in the environment. I felt like a burglar, sneaking around in someone's home, constantly trying not to spook something out of its cozy little nest or den. We marched through the grassland in a semi-single-file line, and I kept one eye on the ground to avoid tripping over a crevice or stepping on a snake, and with the other eye, I kept count of zebras and impalas. Then it was eyes back down to ensure my balance. Along we traveled, eyes up, eyes down; eyes up, eyes down.

Our diligence was rewarded early on when we spotted a female black rhino with her calf. It was incredibly exciting, but we also had to remember to keep our distance since we were on foot and without the protection of the jeep. My nervous energy and uneasy feeling weren't subsiding, so I tried to talk myself down. "Relax, Jan," I thought. "We're not in Brazil with thousands of snakes." Of course, there are snakes in Africa, and all six varieties are venomous, but the sheer numbers and varieties were far less than what I'd already dealt with in South America.

Besides, I was dressed in full gear, with ankle hiking boots, snake guards up to my knees, cargo pants, and a safari vest that John Wayne would covet if he were alive. In addition to its seventeen pockets, I also wore my camera around my neck and a backpack strapped over my shoulders. Having taken stock of my security measures, I finally started to relax a bit. The group was moving quickly because even though the rhino was some distance behind us, she was moving in closer. As I took a hurried step, Solomon suddenly brought his rifle out in front of him, stepped toward me, and plunged the barrel at the ground. With a sweeping motion, he swept a snake off to the side right before I would have stepped on it.

My instincts had been right! Bill and I looked at each other and shook our heads, still trying to be as quiet as possible. I kept making my way forward, trying not to think too hard about what could have happened. Could it have been a green viper, the deadliest of Africa's snakes? We were in a grassy field, after all. Realizing that I wasn't doing a very good job of not thinking too hard about it, I made more of an effort and consciously chose not to ask about the snake. Sometimes not knowing is better.

I sent up a silent thank-you and continued on vigilantly. Of course, I was a bit unnerved, and I just couldn't shake that feeling of impending doom. I joked with Bill about how exciting it was to go to Africa and narrowly miss the kiss of death, and followed up by saying, "I don't think being so quiet is such a good idea. I think we'll end up startling the animals more this way." He nodded and shrugged in a way that said, "Yeah, but we gotta go with the plan."

Eventually, we took a quick break to drink out of our water bottles while surrounded by grazing gazelles, impalas, and zebras. "Okay," Solomon said. "Now we can talk." Over his shoulder about 30 meters was a tree with wide overhanging limbs that provided a nice girth of shade. As I looked up at Solomon, he appeared to have grown horns, one protruding from either side of his head. Actually, it was a large cape buffalo some distance behind him, and I was at exactly the right angle to see the illusion. While it's funny in retrospect, at the time I silently brought my fingers up to my lips and shook my head "no" to let Solomon know that perhaps we should keep silent a bit longer. I pointed behind him, and when he turned to see the enormous animal, his eyes got huge and nearly bulged out of his head. He gave me a thumbs up and also placed a finger to his lips in what I took to be the universal sign for "Oh, my god, don't make a sound or we're all going to die!"

Solomon waved us on, and once we'd gotten a safe distance between us and the Cape buffalo, it was finally okay to speak. "That was a close one!" Solomon exclaimed. "A lone male buffalo is the most dangerous thing of all." That was not necessarily what I needed to hear in my already-agitated, highly freaked out state. Things seemed to just keep getting scarier and scarier, and we'd only been out for about an hour.

"Does anyone else think this is pretty dangerous?" I whispered to Bill. Solomon noticed that we'd stopped and asked if we needed to mark our territory, which a less-than subtle code for "go to the bathroom." I told him I would wait since I wasn't interested in getting caught with my pants down should we encounter some other terrifying creature. Everybody got a good laugh at that visual, but I was still feeling pretty jumpy. I expressed my concern to Bill. "I don't have a good feeling about this. I don't want to sneak up, scare a bunch of warthogs, and have them turn on me!" He understood my concern but then got distracted by a nice find of elephant dung to be examined and recorded on his clipboard.

We walked on, trying not to lose count of the herd of Thompson gazelles we were monitoring at that point. The landscape changed, transitioning from open ground with scattered trees to dense foliage and bush. From a small area of bushes about four meters ahead, an entire family of eight warthogs sprang forth without warning. The group scurried away from us, a piglet tagging behind, its little legs almost a blur with how fast they were moving.

I held my breath for a moment to make sure I wasn't going to lose control of my bowels. Checking in with of all my bodily functions, I felt incredibly grateful that the warthogs had been startled and scared rather than disgruntled and murderous.

"Are you kidding me?!" I looked around at each of my peers. "I do not like this, and I am not so sure this is the way we ought to go about doing this. We shouldn't be sneaking up on these animals!"

"You were right about that one," Bill conceded.

I continued. "I do not have a good feeling about this." My eyes darted back and forth trying to detect any wildlife that might be lurking behind a rock, planning to drop out of a tree, or stalking us in the distance. I was now so far beyond high alert status that I wouldn't have been surprised if an elephant charged us out of thin air.

The group walked on, the silence occasionally broken by the gleeful discovery of some petrified elephant poop. Our treasures were surely untold.

With my next step, I was whisked from reality into what felt like a dream. I clearly saw a vision in my mind. In that vision, a lion jumped out from behind a tree, pounced on Kathy, and dragged her across the plains. Just as quickly, the image was gone, leaving me wondering what the hell my brain had just conjured. I looked around and saw that we had spread out a bit, and that Kathy was a few meters behind the rest of us.

"I think we should get closer together," I announced. "Where is Kathy? She needs to be by me." I waved her over to me and told her I'd like for us to stay closer to each other. I was probably being paranoid and had obviously gotten myself worked up, but I was going with it. We crossed a small dirt road and came to a thicket of large thistle bushes with a skinny path leading through the dense plant life.

Hailey and Solomon walked abreast down the path with him on the left. Kathy and I followed the same way, with her on the left. Bill was quite a ways off checking the outer boundaries of this bush area for more dung. Suddenly, Solomon stopped dead in his tracks, so abruptly, in fact that Kathy and I almost bumped into him and Hailey. He turned to us and whispered.

"Run."

It is a miracle of design and nature how fast the brain can take in, process, and react to information. The number of thoughts I had in less than a second is astronomical. Solomon was pointing to the right, and my body did as it was told, already fully understanding that this was a life or death situation. You're often told not to run in the wild, that it makes you look like prey in a scene out of *Jurassic Park*. But, when it comes down to fight or flight, your instincts know what's up. I turned hard to my right, using full force to push myself off like from a runner's starting block. *What the hell is it?* my brain somehow had the capacity to wonder, despite my body's current attempt to keep them both alive. *A warthog or a buffalo?*

I didn't see or hear anything at first; we were just trying to reach the thicket. On my third step, though, I heard it.

Oh, shit! my internal voice raged. *It's a lion!*

Its roar was so loud that my blood vessels vibrated. *A lion! We are being chased by a lion! I can't outrun a lion!* My mind started to play recordings of the various defense moves and takedowns I'd learned in order to deal with aggressive psych patients. *The lion's got the element of surprise on his side,* I thought. *I can't zig-zag my way out of this. I can't roll backwards and get away.* I felt so weighed down by my boots, camera, and the safari vest that I'd earlier thought John Wayne would have been jealous over. Well, he could have it. I sure didn't remember him having this problem in *Hatari*. Of course, he also had a jeep and his own rifle.

The lion seemed to have built up an incredible amount of inertia. Each time its paws struck the dirt, I could feel the vibrations in my body. Despite the fact that it sounded as if a freight train were on my heels, I could hear a few other sounds, one of which was the rustle of another person running near me. I had about ten steps into my sprint at that point, and I knew that in the next second or two the lion would pounce, and it would be me or the other person.

I couldn't...I wouldn't look. I didn't want to see the

animal take that leap at me, nor did I want to know who its other option was. Instead, I needed every bit of momentum to propel myself forward and into the next thicket of bushes. At this point, I wasn't yet considering my death. First thing's first, after all, and I needed to brace myself for the attack.

What came next was a thud. I turned around, with my hat brim partially blocking my vision to the left. What I could see despite my hat being askew was that the lion was on top of Kathy. She was face down on the ground, covering her head with her arms. In an instant, the lion was off of her and gone. Everything was surreal, and my thoughts were still being processed at an almost incomprehensible speed as I took a few precious seconds to determine what to do next.

Should I go back and apply medical care to Kathy? Do I retrieve her? If I did, there was a good chance I would be killed by the lion. My mind, perhaps in a desperate attempt at self-preservation, flashed pictures of my children and family at me in rapid succession. *Right now, I am alive.* I didn't know how safe I was or for how long, but I was pretty certain I was safer than Kathy.

But I was also a nurse. I couldn't just ignore what was happening to her. Again, I was inundated with images of my children. *Fuck,* I thought, *I may not see them again!* Time had slowed to the point where I was able to recognize what was likely to happen next. If I went back for Kathy, I was probably going to die. But, how could I just leave her out there? I sent out a silent "I love you" as I found my resolve. I prayed that my children would understand, I prayed that they would be OK without me, and I prayed that their lives would be beautiful and fulfilled even though I would not be there to see it.

As I ran back toward where Kathy lay, I asked whatever powers might be listening to please protect us. My heart was beating hard and fast, and my body was so full of adrenaline that it seemed as if it would ooze out of my pores. Each of my senses was so heightened that I could have sworn I was having an out-of-body experience. Still, I could hear the sounds of my belongings clinking in my backpack, feel the camera against my chest, register the sound and feel of my clothes as they rustled with every movement.

When I arrived, Kathy was trying to crawl away on her elbows. It seemed impossible, but no blood was spurting, a truly good sign. My eyes scanned her up and down while my hands busily worked over her body like search dogs sniffing for a clue. I couldn't believe it when I counted all four of her limbs still attached.

"Are you okay?" I asked her. It seemed like a fairly ridiculous question to ask someone who you just watched get attacked by a wild lion, but my training had kicked in, and that is the first thing you ask in a medical situation. "Can you move? Can you hear me?" I continued to asses her.

Kathy started to moan, and I saw that her back left pocket was torn halfway off. As I took in each detail, my mind was still racing with questions about the lion. Where was it? When would it come back? Was everyone else OK? I looked under the hole in her pocket and saw a gash about two inches wide on the top of her buttocks. She told me she thought she was okay, as she attempted to orient herself and find her glasses.

I started to babble. "I can't believe it! I can't believe it! You can move!" Everything about the situation left me incredulous, but before I could continue my stream-of-consciousness rant, I heard a growl. I turned to look over my left shoulder and saw the lioness. She was about ten meters away, back in front of the bush she originally leapt from.

"We have to move!" I urged Kathy. She asked me to give her a minute, apparently oblivious that we were still in incredible danger. I looked back at the lioness, making direct eye contact for a brief moment. In response, she let out a roar that made my ears ring, her mouth so wide that I could have fit a basketball in it. She pulled her ears back and readied herself to pounce.

"There's no time!" I shouted, grabbing Kathy by the back of her pants and pulling her to her feet. As I dragged her along, attempting to run, she threatened to pass out. She begged me to let her rest. "No!" I told her. "Go ahead and pass out, because we aren't stopping!" Just as she went limp, Bill came running and lifted the other side of her. He hugged her, relieved that she was alive, but I intervened shouting, "We have to GO!"

Hailey arrived running from another direction. I reached out to touch her arm, as if I needed reassurance that she was real. The group of us started to run, terrified, asking each other what the hell had just happened.

We were all speaking at once, with me asking where the lion had gone and searching for a place where we could hide. The trees were too small. Could a bush would afford enough protection until help arrived? For her part, Kathy was rambling, in shock, asking if we'd seen how beautiful the lioness was as we ran down the road supporting her under her arms.

We finally stopped, looking around in all directions. I had no idea if we'd gotten far enough away. Kathy was chatting along in her shock, trying to convince us that she was fine. "Just sew up my pants and continue on," she suggested. I assessed her wound more thoroughly. She wasn't bleeding from the top of the claw mark, but there was blood coming from the lower part. I pulled out my antiseptic wipes and packed the wound.

Kathy wanted to know if I had gotten a picture of the lion. She asked me, "Did you mark it down, Jan, that we saw a lion?" It was amazing to me that even if she hadn't been in shock, these are the very same questions Kathy would have asked. This seventy-something woman was passionate about animals and truly wanted to protect them. "I'm pretty sure I won't forget to, Kathy," I responded, assessing the other members of our group for injuries. Hailey resembled a porcupine due to all of the two-inch thorns sticking out of her. Solomon had thrown her into a bush opposite from where the lion was right before she saw it leap over Solomon to chase after us.

We were all attempting to piece together what had happened, asking who had seen what. Hailey said that after the lion finished the attack and retreated to a bush, she was forced to run in front of it in order to get to us. We all hugged one another over and over and agreed that our guardian angels had been watching over us that day. It was nothing short of a miracle to have survived a lion chase.

As we stood comparing details, Solomon arrived running. His eyes were huge as he held out his hand, revealing three bullets. "The rifle jammed! The rifle jammed!" he yelled, obviously still in the grip of what had just transpired.

"What the hell?" I yelled back. "Don't you guys check these rifles out in the morning?" He assured me that they did. But as I was tending to Kathy and the lioness was poised for the second attack, the rifle had jammed anyway. I was stunned. Why hadn't she pounced? Why was I still alive?

Solomon used the cell phone to call for help while I continued to assess the patients. Poor Hailey looked like a pin cushion and probably felt about the same. The lot of us were hyper-verbal, talking fast and loud to keep up with our racing thoughts. Solomon explained what had set the series of events in motion. As we were approaching the original bush on the path, Solomon caught sight of the lioness sleeping with two, maybe three, cubs. There was little doubt that she would attack, so he had told us to run. Hailey was in the direct line of sight of the lion, so he threw her into the opposite bush.

He didn't try to fire when the lion was on Kathy for fear of hitting the woman instead of the animal, so he had instead struck the predator with his gun butt, which is why it retreated the first time. My hat had been blocking me from seeing Solomon there. It was when I went back for Kathy that he had tried to shoot, but the rifle jammed, and he ended up yelling at the lion and waving the gun at her.

I discretely informed Solomon that Kathy was more severely injured than she realized and needed medical attention. He assured me that the assistant director had been apprised of our location, but it still felt like an eternity before we finally saw the jeep come barreling toward us. We were all so grateful for that sight, and when Joseph got out of the car, he was assailed by all versions of the story at the same time. I let him know that we needed to get Kathy to the hospital.

"Oh, I'm okay. I will heal," she told us whippersnappers.

"She was a bit heavy on me though," she said to Joseph. This elderly woman had just survived a lion attack, and her only complaint was that the cat was "a bit heavy!" Unbelievable!

I didn't want to alarm her, so I casually suggested that she needed to get an assessment and maybe a few shots to prevent infection. As I helped her into the jeep, I got a better idea of the severity of the injury. As she stepped up, the lesion opened more. The gash went through the fatty tissue and muscles, creating a deep, gaping wound. Blood began to gush out. I turned to Hailey, who wore a terrified look, and asked her to get my sweatshirt out of the backpack I was still wearing. I told Kathy I was going to use it to prop her up and keep her from putting pressure on the left buttock, leaving out the part about how I was also going to apply as much pressure as possible to slow the extensive blood loss.

I checked Kathy's pulse every five minutes as we bounced our way to the hospital. "Keep drinking water and talking, and everyone will be fine," I repeated over and over, trying to keep all of our adrenalized selves from slipping too far into shock. The conversation centered around each of us sharing what we saw and felt and experienced from our points of view.

Kathy made the 30-minute drive quite well, although I was concerned the amount of blood she'd lost already. It had soaked just about through the sweatshirt by the time we got to the hospital in Nanyuki. She was wheeled into the emergency room of the private, rural institution. At first it seemed that none of the medical staff really recognized the severity of the wound. It was incomprehensible to them that an elderly woman had survived a full-on lion attack, and so they assumed it was just a scratch.

I knew that the care in a rural African hospital would differ from what one would expect in the States, and I did my best to take a step back rather than become the bossy, know-it-all Westerner in the room. Still, the situation was eye-opening. Supplies were minimally stocked, but the building seemed to be clean and structurally sound. I was able to assist with her care by applying pressure to the wound while the other nurses cut her pants away and brought out a few dressing supplies.

It was good to see that they got Kathy a first round of rabies shots, but I was concerned that they didn't start her on IV fluids. There was a real risk of her going into deep shock due to the trauma and blood loss. I tried to explain that the wound needed to be packed, but the nurses instead taped some gauze over it. Not surprisingly, it bled through quickly. The only thing I could find to pack it was a wad of cotton, so I grabbed it up and yelled at the nurses to bring me more. When they saw what was happening, they began to better understand that this was a more emergent situation than they originally thought. "Oh, no!" they said. "We need to stop this! Let the doctor know!"

I did my best to be understanding, recognizing that they were doing their best with the information they had. My hand was beginning to shake, not just from applying constant pressure to the wound, but because my own shock was starting to set in. I was indoors now, feeling safer, and my adrenaline was beginning to abate, taking with it the fight-or-flight instinct. The next step in this natural progression would be to fall into shock. It would not be much longer before I buckled under the reality of what had happened that day. *Hang on*, I told myself. *Focus on being a nurse for right now, and you can fall apart later.* Holding on to what little grip I still had, I suggested that we start IV fluids and get Kathy's vitals while waiting for the doctor to arrive.

The entire medical situation was so far out of my normal realm of operation that it was a bit disorienting. It was a situation where things should have been so familiar, and yet, the actual functions and activities felt like they had been turned ten or fifteen degrees off center. For example, the few supplies the hospital had could not be kept in the rooms, both because there weren't enough to stock all the rooms, and also because they would be vulnerable to theft. The hospital didn't have air conditioning, and so the windows were kept open to allow for a breeze. Because of the warm temperatures, the saline solution was kept in the refrigerator. In order to warm it up to room temperature for use, the nurses submerged the bag in a bucket of warm water. And then we waited.

Everything took longer than I would have expected. There were no immediate responses to my requests. Even taking Kathy's vitals required waiting for someone to retrieve the machine used for that purpose from somewhere else in the hospital.

When the doctor arrived, I explained the situation. He injected some Lidocaine, an anesthetic, into Kathy's wound—the first pain relief she'd had since the attack happened. I grabbed her hands and told her to squeeze if she needed to and positioned my face in front of hers to try to keep her calm and distracted while the doctor conducted his exam. He told me to take a look, and when I did, I saw that he had fit his entire fist into the wound. Surgery was required, and the muscles would have to be stitched up in layers.

Kathy had gone white and clammy. She was moaning in pain as a result of the extensive exam. "Get those fluids in her now!" I commanded. "And what are her vitals?!" Her blood pressure had dropped to 67/40, and she was clearly losing consciousness. Once she had some fluids and her pain was being better managed, I was able to update Hailey, Bill, and Geoffrey, who had been waiting in the hallway. As she underwent surgery, we walked across the street to a little café to eat and talk. My career had given me plenty of insight into how important it is to talk about trauma in order to work through and lessen the potential effects of Post-Traumatic Stress Disorder.

The surgery lasted a couple of hours, and since Kathy was well-sedated for the night, I returned to the camp where a whirlwind of phone calls, concern, and speculation were underway. Because of my medical education, I was able to play an important part in answering questions coming from Kathy's family in the US and Earthwatch's London headquarters, not to mention the other volunteers. When I told the rest of our group about the vision I'd had right before the attack, their response was, "Tell us next time!"

By nightfall, I was exhausted. I wanted to cry and be held; but I wanted my family and friends from home to do it. My volunteer teammates were wonderful and supportive, but I didn't feel like I could really fall apart with any of them. Those of us involved in the incident were struggling with it. I couldn't decide if I should call my family or not, since I had three weeks left in Africa and didn't want them to worry. In fact, all of us struggled with this decision. On the one hand, we had just faced our own mortality, and something like that tends to make you want to reach out to your loved ones. On the other hand, what was the point of worrying them over something that was over and done?

Poor Hailey went to bed with a flashlight on but was unable to sleep, her mind racing all night with "what if" scenarios. For example, what if the lion had attacked Solomon, the person with the rifle and the cell phone? This thought hadn't occurred to me yet, and when she brought it up, the implications left me dumbfounded. We were so lucky in the way things turned out, and we were blessed by Solomon's bravery.

Sleep didn't come easily for me, either. I kept hearing the lion's roar over and over. Some mild PTSD symptoms persisted, too. I couldn't seem to walk past the perimeter of the camp where the foliage got a little denser. Even when I went back to Nairobi, I would find myself walking in the middle of the roads when I was off the main streets. I could not bring myself to walk along sidewalks if there were bushes lining them. It would take some time and distance before I would feel truly recovered.

The morning after the attack, I was anxious to get back to the hospital and check on Kathy. Earthwatch was sending someone from London to deal with the situation and oversee her care. Amid these utterly strange circumstances, the organization did an amazing job of providing support and keeping us all updated. Before I left for the hospital, though, I decided to call two friends in the US to let them know what had happened. I was pretty sure I was going to have to call my family, knowing I'd be in huge trouble if I waited to get home to share what had happened. I thought that perhaps I could gauge my friends' responses, as well as my own, before reaching out to my family.

I recounted the tale with both Lori and Allen, still in some shock over what had happened. It was surreal to find myself saying things like, "Well, I just wanted to let you know I got chased by a lion. Oh, no, I'm good. I jammed my knee, but I'm good."

Just hearing about the event was enough to leave my friends and family daunted. They needed time to process the information and their feelings about it, so we determined that I would call them back in 24 hours, after they'd had time to sit with the story and recognize what questions they had about it. Kathy also found these conversation difficult as she called home to talk to her children. "The last thing my son said to me before I left for Africa was, 'Don't get eaten by a lion, Mom!'" she told me, with a worried, if somewhat amused, look on her face.

Of course, I had a lot to sort through and internalize. What I found was that everything sort of fell into place—each event, change of plans, and thought process lining up perfectly for me to be in the right place at the right time. I came to the conclusion that this experience was why my plans had been disrupted when I was scheduling the trip. After all, I was originally supposed to be on a completely different expedition and not have even met this group of volunteers. Months before, on the other side of the world, the Universe had already set this entire row of dominos up and starting knocking them down one by one with me ending up in this exact place.

There was also that vision right before the attack— the one in which I saw Kathy being dragged away by a lion, the one that prompted me to have her move closer and join the group. Did that small change in the course of events affect the outcome? Whatever the factors that caused me to be in that place at that time, they seemed to have aligned just right. In my heart, I felt that I had been maneuvered into place to help and protect Kathy when she needed it. It was a bizarre honor, but an honor nonetheless.

Kathy's family was so gracious about my involvement, calling me her guardian angel. I, on the other hand, was marveling over the repeated instances of visions before and during my travels. The track record of them coming to pass was undeniable. It was a little difficult to accept, but the fact of the matter was that my entire quest had been built on the desire to put my theories about such things to the test. As a result, I was finding that I could rely on me, that I could—and should—listen to my own intuition and inner knowing, because it was clearly capable of guiding me in the right directions.

Geoffrey and I made our way in to Nanyuki later that morning. Kathy was a vegetarian, and I was concerned about her getting enough protein in her diet. After so much muscle damage, loss of blood, and surgery, she would need a lot of protein for her body to repair and rebuild. We stopped at a grocery store so I could buy some nuts, cheese, and avocados. I smiled a bit as I picked out the green fruit. Kathy and I loved the avocados in Kenya, so perfectly ripe and huge that one could practically feed a family of four. It was a relief to realize that we could continue enjoying them together. Had things gone a different way the day before, I might have spent the rest of my life reminded of my dear, late friend Kathy every time I ate an avocado.

The entire time I was in the store, I felt strange. Here I was, alive and grocery shopping the day after being chased by a lion. It was surreal and eerie. I looked around the store and thought, *I'm probably the only person here who can say that*. I wasn't looking at it as some sort of elevated status for myself, rather I felt like it made me somehow odd, different. Considering we were in Kenya and surrounded by wildlife, it wasn't unthinkable that others had dealt with some large carnivore or another; but it turns out that being chased by a lion and surviving the attack is a pretty big deal—even in Kenya.

The four of us involved in the incident were told again and again what a miracle it was that no one died. All lions, we were told, attack to kill. And, of course, a female with cubs posed the ultimate threat. Lions don't try to scare you off with a warning, and they don't back down. Kenyans believe that if it is your time to die, it will happen; and if it's not your time, it won't. "It was not your time to die," the locals told us many times during the next week. "You have special angels."

Standing in that grocery store, I did feel somehow "other," and it wasn't just because of my light skin and hair. It was about the profound realizations that were going on inside of me. Some people don't believe in the supernatural or spiritual intervention, but I had grown to believe in the signs that were clearly happening around me. I also believe in putting your best foot forward every day to create the kind of energy that you want in your life. We are surrounded by energy—in fact we are made up of it, even on a cellular level. Whether you are looking at our bodies, nature, or outer space, the universe is comprised of energy. Chemistry is what creates, but it is the essence of that creation that is so mind boggling, mystifying, significant, powerful, and illuminating. I draw from that a feeling of something incredibly powerful existing outside of us. It is that essences that I call "spirit."

My spirituality is based on the belief that something intangible and unseen exists outside of myself. I see this energy as the beautiful source of all of creation. It is the mother of all mothers. Through trial and error, I have learned that if I just let go and accept the energy, if I believe in its beauty and allow it to create, things become far greater than I could have ever imagined.

Of course, recent events also had me contemplating the more fearsome aspects of existence, such as why evil exists. We all know that for every action there is a reaction. For a positive there is a negative, up has down. Right and wrong, love and hate, the existence of one reveals the existence of the other. My focus is on the positive, and it has worked for me. There is a television commercial that always makes me smile when it gets to the catchphrase: "It's not weird if it works!" Spirituality is very personal. Each of us is unique, and therefore our spiritual beliefs are, too. There is no right or wrong when you listen to your heart and attempt to become a better person by growing within yourself, helping others, and being a steward of the planet.

I wrestled then with these deep thoughts, as I still do today. I had run into the lions' den, and while I had come out physically unscathed, there were spiritual awakenings happening. Perhaps this is how astronauts feel upon returning to earth after orbiting the planet or walking on the moon.

I sat with Kathy and provided oversight on her care until the representative from Earthwatch arrived. The hospital was very different from what I was used to in the States, but it was clean, and the care was good. The atmosphere was calm and quiet, and fresh air filtered in through open windows. I had seen plenty of medical facilities in Kenya that were little more than huts constructed of cardboard and wood scraps, so I was pleased that we had such a nice place for Kathy to be treated for her injuries. Some of the medical techniques used were not as advanced as those back home, so I kept a vigilant eye out and brought extra alcohol wipes.

Kathy and I kept each other company for most of that day, sharing stories from our respective lives and growing closer. Lucy, the representative from Earthwatch, arrived and became a hub and go-to person for everyone from the medical staff to the volunteers. There were many, many layers involved that went beyond simply making sure Kathy got proper care. The organization itself brought with it the need to consult with their medical advisors, legal advisors, and administrators. There was the hospital staff to consider, Ol Pejeta Conservancy and their security, Kathy's family, Dr. Geoffrey Wahungu, and of course all of us at the camp. Lucy was amazing, and I was absolutely impressed with the care that Earthwatch provided for Kathy.

The next day, Hailey, Bill, and I joined a few other volunteers to check on a particular lot of acacia trees. Solomon went with us, and we were all so happy to see him. There were lots of hugs and sharing of details and perspectives on what had come to be known as the Lion Incident. Not surprisingly, Hailey, Bill, and I were fairly jumpy out in the field. We were far too aware of how the bushes around us could camouflage large animals just as easily as small ones.

Sure enough, as we were measuring an acacia tree, a lone male Cape buffalo made his way out from behind a bush. Just yesterday I had been told that this was the animal that was "most dangerous of all," which took on an entirely new meaning for me today. I grabbed Joseph and Hailey who were right in front of me. The buffalo looked at us before turning to run the other direction. Hailey and I managed not to curl up in the fetal position, but it did take me a moment to release my death grip on her and Joseph.

I spent much of my time being hyper-vigilant. I was highly distracted, constantly scanning the area for danger, and found it difficult to stay on task. Despite my minimal help with the work, the job finished early, and it was decided we could go for a drive. My first panicked thought was, "No, thanks. I'd like to go back to the camp where it feels a little safer." I didn't share my thoughts out loud, but Hailey and I kept staring at each other in disbelief over this turn of events. Each knew that the other was thinking of wanting only to get the hell out of there, but we also realized that the other volunteers would be unfairly limited if we spoke up.

On the drive, we came across two male lions. They sat, posed as if waiting for us to take their picture. I was not the good kind of excited about this. Perhaps it could be an opportunity to desensitize myself to a PTSD trigger, I thought, forcing myself to look at the animals. I felt physically ill. I was only able to glance at them twice. As the others took the opportunity for a photo shoot, I declined to even get my camera out. Hailey was on the passenger side in the back by the window, the lions just on the other side of the glass. She didn't look at them either. We simply sat in the jeep, silently communicating with one another about the ridiculous luck that brought lions to our path on this, of all days.

We eventually moved on, finding what seemed like a less

terrifying photo op with some rhinos. Things got a bit dicey, though, when a couple of the armored animals lumbered towards us. The jeep had been having some problems with the ignition, and as two of the rhinos grew closer and closer, the vehicle refused to start. They have terrible eyesight, and they were likely more curious than irritated by us, but those are the kinds of things that can change in an instant.

"Let's go," I said, feeling a bit desperate. One of the other volunteers asked why, and I blurted out, "Because it makes me nervous, that's why!" My stomach was queasy, and tears were beginning to well up in my eyes. Clearly, it was going to take some time to work through these emotions, especially while I was still in Kenya. I didn't like putting a damper on other people's enjoyment of their experience, but some things are just outside of our control.

A few days later, the volunteers of the Ol Pejeta Conservancy participated in Community Outreach Day. The Conservancy supported a number of projects for the benefit of the local community, such as supplying computers for the schools that community members could also use in the evenings. Another wonderful gift was water towers for the schools. These provided irrigation so that the students could garden and sell their goods at the market.

The children who attended school considered themselves very fortunate and took their education seriously. The system required parents to pay for their children's education, starting with preschool. Without preschool, kids are not allowed to attend elementary school, even if the parents can afford to pay the tuition. In order to improve access to education, a woman's job training program was established where women learned to spin and hand-dye wool to make beautiful shawls, rugs, and wall hangings.

There was a preschool on the Conservancy property, educating children ranging from two to five years old. Students traveled long distances to attend, some walking a few miles each way with their parents every day for the privilege of going to school. Other parents brought their kids by bicycle, and it was impossible not to compare this to the long "car lines" of big automobiles where parents in the US drop off their own preschoolers for the day.

The preschool building, 25 feet by 15 feet and made of cement blocks, was paid for by the government. The green tin roof was provided by Ol Pejeta Conservancy. The school's two windows were partially boarded up, because glass was just too expensive. It had a makeshift door, pieced together from scraps of wood. Inside was a hard dirt floor, a couple of tables, and a chalkboard.

We visited the school one day in August, which is actually a cooler time in Kenya. The temperature was in the 50s, with wind and rain. The children were dressed as if it were the dead of winter back home. They were layered in clothing and coats that had obviously been worn by other children before them. Despite the worn-out appearance of their clothes, their faces were bright and sunny. The ten children, led by their teacher and a couple of mothers, had been looking forward to the excitement of the day and performed songs and dances for us. Their smiles were brilliant as the performed their moves, and to this day, my smile is just as brilliant when I remember their enthusiasm and joy.

There was no heat source for the classroom, and even wearing my jacket inside, I was cold. When I asked Joseph why the school didn't have windows or a proper door despite having been in operation for ten years, his explanation was simple. "It's not a priority. Money has to be shared with too many." The country's government did its part, and Ol Pejeta did its part, and the result was that there was a classroom and a teacher. I asked how much it would cost for windows and a door. The figure was about $600 US dollars, not much more than purchasing a piece of art as a souvenir from one's African adventures.

And yet, in the ten years that volunteers and tourists had been coming and going, no one ever determined that a door and windows for the preschool was a high enough priority. That, to me, was pretty much unbelievable. Before setting out on my trip, I had put aside some money with the intention of donating it to a cause along the way. I had been sure that I would recognize it when the time came, and boy, did I! I gave Joseph the money and asked that the windows and door be installed as soon as possible because the weather was only going to get colder with more rain in the next few months.

I wasn't there when they were put up, but it was done in short order; and when I got home, I received a letter from Joseph detailing how excited everyone was about the additions to their school. Some of the women spilled tears of joy! He also told me about the next expedition group that came through the Conservancy, ten of whom were from China. He explained to them about the school's new windows and doors and how lucky the children and parents all felt to have real glass windows to keep them dry and warm. The Chinese group talked amongst themselves and donated $100 US each for a total of $1,000. The preschool was able to buy furniture and supplies that would last for years to come.

Sometimes, it's just about making that one small gesture. It's about hearing your own wisdom tell you what's right and following through on it. As I learned, these small acts are akin to tossing a pebble into a pond. The stone sinks after it's broken through the surface, but it also sends out ripples that reach all the way to the shore. I hope to someday go back and visit the little preschool that sits out in the vast lands of Africa.

The black rhino expedition ended with a party at our camp on the last evening. The highlight of the event was that *all* of the volunteers were there, as Kathy had been released from the hospital and was able to stay the night with us. She was unable to fly home just yet because here hemoglobin was too low, but everyone was hopeful that it would only take a few more days for it to rise to levels that meant her bloodstream was being properly oxygenated.

The entire staff was invited to the going-away party, providing a great opportunity for us to gift them with gratuities in order to say "thank you" for all they had done for us. Even the drivers and guards were there, and Solomon was beside himself with joy at seeing Kathy. He was also leaving the next day to have a short visit to reconnect with his wife and family after the harrowing Lion Incident. His brave deeds that day certainly warranted a little respite!

The party was a lot of fun. I remembered back to the first few days at camp and my disappointment at the fact that my team was made of Americans. It had seemed impossible that I would get as close to them as I did with my English mates in Brazil, or even with Doug, my East-Coast Gemini buddy. That worry ended up being misguided, as I certainly did bond with my teammates. Jim and I were especially close, developing a genuine friendship over wine and cheese at the nightly happy hour we established. As a going-away gift, I gave him a wooden rhino carved from a wine bottle cork. He was on the expedition as a present from his family. He'd been intrigued by rhinos for years, and they thought it was the perfect way to wish him a happy 70th birthday.

It is so interesting to look back and realize how much we learned about one another in such a short period of time. Kelly worked at a zoo in Austin, Texas. Bill and Judy were so much fun and were both dedicated to caring for the environment. They had been on many endangered animal expeditions and had brought their nephew Paul along as his high school graduation gift. I secretly suspected that Paul was a prince in disguise, with his polite and grounded demeanor. I loved listening to their adventures around the campfire.

I am sure many adventures awaited the young couple Kim and Eric. His exuberance for life perfectly complemented her more grounded approach. Hailey shared a lot about her family, an incredibly loving and supportive bunch. She and Meredith, a volunteer from California, often discussed their love of horses, describing the animal's sixth sense and sharing stories of how they are used therapeutically. Meredith was a great advocate for young people through her work as a high school dean, always encouraging them to aspire to great things. Rebecca also worked with high schoolers as a science teacher. Patience and intelligence exuded from her, both traits that were helpful in her hobby of bird watching. It was inspiring to learn about how she and others like her are out in the world working to protect our fabulous flying friends.

And, of course, there was Kathy. What a truly amazing, giving, and undeniably brave woman. Considering all that she went through, this 72-years-young woman never complained or backed down. Back in the North Carolina Mountains, she and a friend oversaw a bear education center. I knew there was a reason my plans had to be changed on this expedition, but if I had realized what was in store for me, I probably wouldn't have signed on!

What a ride it was. I was absolutely blessed by the wonderful people with whom I was able to share this time. The volunteers, the staff, the Kenyans themselves were all a dynamic part of a transformative life experience. There is forever a place in my heart that is shaped like Africa.

CHAPTER 7

Uganda

The gorilla is one of the closest "relatives" of humans, sharing 95-99% of our DNA. Mountain gorillas are on the verge of extinction, with little more than an estimated 600 left on earth. Adult males, often referred to as silverbacks, span from five-and-a-half to six feet tall, and weigh in anywhere between 400 to 700 pounds. These animals have very long arms and typically move by knuckle-walking.

A group of gorillas is known as a troop and is usually headed up by a silverback who leads and protects a number of females and their offspring. The silverback, so named because of the patch of silver along a mature male's back, keeps busy managing the affairs of the troop. He decides where they will go and when, leading his troop to food and safety, and will use his brute strength and large canine teeth to fight to the death to protect them from danger.

Each night, members of the troop build nests, usually on the ground, out of tree branches and leaves. Babies sleep in their mothers' nests until about age three when they start to build their own. A female typically has her first baby during her tenth year, with a new offspring following about every four years after that. This long period between births allows for the mother to focus her care on one infant at a time, which is necessary for their survival. In the wild, gorillas usually live between 35 and 40 years.

The animals are very social, with strong bonds developed between the silverback and his females. Grooming, playing, and living together reinforce these bonds. For their part, unrelated females tend to be aggressive toward each other, vying for the attention of the leader. The makeup of the troop affects the behavior of the younger males. If there are multiple males in a mixed-sex group, the boys tend to compete with one another and don't develop strong social bonds. In all-male groups, however, they get along well.

Gorillas have deep, soulful eyes that make it easy to anthropomorphize them. However, their physical characteristics and genetic makeup aren't the only things they have in common with humankind. For example, gorillas communicate vocally, making about 25 different noises that can serve to get their points across to one another. There have also been some famous gorillas, like Koko, who have learned and used a considerable amount of sign language to communicate with humans.

Like people, gorillas can laugh, and they grieve, as well. It has also been found that they can think about both the future and the past. One of the clearest signs of their intelligence *is the fact they can make and use tools, something that sets them apart from almost the entire animal kingdom. Perhaps the most strikingly "human" trait is that gorillas actually develop cultures that differ from one another, with different rituals and preferences.*

While the mountain gorilla is listed by the International Union for the Conservation of Nature as Critically Endangered, it is not the only one of its kind facing extinction. The western gorilla is also Critically Endangered, and the eastern gorilla is categorized as Endangered. As is so often the case, the majority of the threat these animals face is a direct result of human activity, whether it's destruction of the gorillas' habitat or hunting them for trophies. A number of organizations have stepped in to try and save these animals, and much attention was brought to the issue with the 1988 film Gorillas in the Mist. *Still, the population continues to decline, and it is quite likely that my generation will be the last to share the planet with our long-lost cousins.*

The little commuter plane touched down on the runway at Entebbe International Airport in Uganda. The airport sits near the shores of Lake Victoria, the largest lake in Africa, and second only in size to Lake Superior in the US. The resulting humidity wrapped itself around me like a veil as I stepped from the aircraft and reveled in the warm sunshine. I had been surprised that even though it is on the equator, the 60-degree autumn weather in Kenya had been much cooler than I expected. The mornings had been cool, but by about 11 a.m., it was pleasant with afternoon winds that lasted for a couple of hours.

The Uganda airport was small but modern, and once again I was dazzled by the friendly, beautiful smiles of the other travelers. I met my guide Paul, and we loaded my belongings into his red Land Rover. A handsome, well-educated man in his late twenties, Paul took his travel business and the tourism industry very seriously. It was a win-win for him, as he could show travelers his country, help the economy, and earn his own livelihood doing something he loved.

Like many Ugandans, Paul was darker-skinned than the Kenyans and had an even thicker accent. After a week with him, most of which was spent riding in his Land Rover, I still understood only about half of what he said! It was exhausting to concentrate so hard on lip reading to help me figure out what he was trying to convey when he spoke. Still, Paul was a wonderful guide, very conscientious and always running things by me to make sure I was happy and content. I really enjoyed having the one-on-one time while we traveled about. I learned so much about the culture and politics, and that was while only understanding about 50% of what he said.

We stayed first in the capital city of Kampala. It was an easy drive out in the country with occasional armed security checks. The guards were friendly enough, although I got the sense that they were conducting very serious business and one would not want to mess with these guys. The country was in far better shape than it had been, as it was coming out from under the grueling thumb of decades of rule by Dictator Idi Armin. Uganda had a new president who had chosen to provide safety and security for his people.

The situation wasn't without its threats, though. There was always concern about terrorist activity, and Sudan proved to be a not-so-friendly neighbor. President Museveni was working to help his people prosper, but the specter of corruption still loomed large in the system. Originally, Museveni had vowed to only hold office for four years, but he decided he liked the job and was going to keep it. So much for democracy.

The leader's motorcade passed by us one afternoon. It was exciting; I'd never been that close to any president before. There wasn't a lot of fanfare, though, the president preferring to travel around the country with just a few vehicles. Museveni kept a military presence all throughout Uganda, but it was exceptionally more prevalent in Kampala due to its size and a population of more than one and a half million. It is unfortunate that this military presence was necessary, and it was quite an awakening for me to understand that the people here lived under such threat from outside forces. Greed, power, the desire to take what is not yours—to kill for it—is a poison to humankind and the planet.

I am often asked which of the places I visited during my travels was my favorite. Each country holds its own special memories for me. In Brazil, it was being with the jaguar cubs, meeting my wonderful English friends, and visiting the Iguaçu Falls. While in Greece, it was being in the lovely town of Vonitsa and being surrounded by dolphins out in the Mediterranean. In Kenya, it was the beautiful warm citizens, the wild life...and *surviving* that wildlife! In each of these countries, I felt that I had some sort of idea of what to expect.

That was not the case with Uganda. This country was the biggest surprise and brought an incredible new awareness to me during my quest. I was rendered speechless when Paul and I entered the outskirts of Kampala. In my mind, I was prepared for a poor, third-world country; but the reality of it was a whole different ballgame. I was stunned by the sheer magnitude of humanity. There were just so many people.

It seemed to me that it was like being in the crowded streets of Hong Kong or India, but the space was so much more confined. People literally walked shoulder to shoulder. Bicycles carried bodies on the seats, handlebars, and fenders, and they were packed in so close to the cars that they could easily reach in and tap a driver on the shoulder if they'd wanted. Motorcycles weaved in and out carrying four passengers. Pedestrians ambled through traffic made up of vehicles stuffed with people like a clown car at the circus. This all took place on a road that purported to be two lanes, although there were no actual lanes defined. Basically, it was an entangled free-for-all.

I asked Paul what would happen if there was an accident. How would medical services get through? He said that someone would put an injured party in their own vehicle, but getting them to help would take some time. The traffic congestion went on for miles in all directions, inching along through the dirtiest, smokiest air I had ever seen. In Kenya, the towns were lined with garbage, and small fires were in constant use, not just to burn the trash, but also for heating and cooking. The borders of Kampala were so far beyond this, and I feared that with my asthma, I would not last a day in the area.

There are no garbage services or sewer systems in the towns that lie outside of Kampala. It was near dusk, and everything blended together in shades of gray and dirt brown. Massive numbers of shops and homes were intertwined, and even compared to the makeshift structures I saw in Kenya, these were woeful. *This is definitely the third world*, I thought, amidst the unceasing movement that would have resembled an ant farm had it not been for the fact that at least ant farms are neat and organized. This was massive, polluted chaos that churned and begat itself in this manner every day of the month, every month of the year, year after year; and no one here knew of any other way.

We reached downtown Kampala by early evening, and the difference between it and the outlying areas could not have been starker. It was so much like any other large city. There was a business center with important-looking buildings and neighborhoods that ranged from affluent to I-wouldn't-go-there-after-dark. My hotel was lovely and afforded a spectacular hilltop view. I sat in my room, drinking Drambuie, my head whirling with the juxtaposition of what I had seen. Images crowded one another in my mind, fighting for the chance for me to make sense of them.

I kept telling myself that this is what I had wanted to experience. I had wanted to know the reality of life in a third-world country. Quick on the heels of that thought was, "Be careful what you wish for!" My adrenaline was pounding as I became distressingly aware of my skin color, of my sex, of the fact that I was traveling in this potentially dangerous place alone. I was overwhelmed and fearful, and I kept wondering how I was going to weather my time in Uganda. The fact was, I had to consider this because this was real, not some documentary I was watching on television. I was tasting it, feeling it, and living it.

I picked up the phone and called my ex-husband. He and I had watched those documentaries together over the years and had many discussions about the plight of these countries. I shared my experience with him and grappled with the reality that was now a part of my own personal awareness. While he may have seemed like an odd choice for me to reach out to, he was the person I thought of who might have an inkling of what I was feeling. It turned out to be the right choice. We had a great conversation, and he helped me channel my nervous energy and feelings of isolation. I managed to get some sleep and woke nervous but more centered.

My first planned adventure in Uganda took me to the Nile River via a rafting company that operated nearby. Along with about twenty other outdoor enthusiasts, I spent the day riding the rapids of the famed Nile River. This was the river of Cleopatra, the source of fertile soil that sustained human life from nearly the beginning, the byway that allowed for cultural and economic expansion throughout the ancient world. Rafting it was a thrill, but the poverty experienced by those along its shores would always taint the memory for me. From the boat, we saw small children wearing clothes that were basically a collection of holes held together by a few strips of fabric.

Many places Paul and I stopped for breaks brought these children running to me, often with outstretched hands. "Give me money." "You have a dollar?" They were certainly blunt, but there was no sense of disrespect in their requests. It was a way of life and a means for survival. There were no hard feelings, no personal affront taken if you declined. The children realized that the answer would always be "no," if they didn't ask, so why not make the request and see what happened?

Most likely, these children had been taught that tourists from other countries were rich and could afford to give their money away. While many tourists would beg to differ, the fact of the matter is that we often can. We have the luxury and choice about where to travel. While we're there, we can pick and choose our accommodations and our food. We have no shortage of choices. The only choice these children had was to ask or not to ask. When you put it that way, the answer is fairly obvious.

Just as so many of the people in Uganda suffer, so too do a number of the animals. I had come to the country for the purpose of observing one of these species. Two days' journey by automobile brought me to my next lodging as I made my way to The Impenetrable Forest near the border of Rwanda and my dream of seeing the silverback gorilla with my own eyes.

Staying at the hostel gave me yet another perspective on life in Uganda. Things there moved at a slow, peaceful pace, and we were able to unwind a bit as Paul shared a variety of cultural and geographical information. Of course, what he shared was only from his perspective, and there are so many political, societal, and historical factors at play, that it's impossible to be completely objective. He explained tribal differences in the area and how inter-tribal marriage had become more common recently than in the past. There was considerably less fighting among the tribes now, but that didn't remove much of the underlying distrust the groups had of one another.

According to Paul, when choosing a wife, the men would show preference to women with lighter skin. The children from these unions would hopefully be lighter and enjoy cultural and economic advantages because of it. I couldn't quite process that information and was mortified. "You mean to tell me you are all prejudiced against your own kind?" I asked Paul. He explained that black was beautiful, but lighter skin represented a higher level in the social structure.

"That's crazy!" I blurted out, joking, "Being white isn't all it's cracked up to be. I mean, we're all trying to get tanned because we like the darker look!" I was still incredulous, and Paul and I had a very interesting conversation in which I shared some of my views about skin color, national identity, and social standing in the US. Of course, I had grown up understanding that racial prejudice and inequality are unfortunately still a part of the American culture, but I had never considered that this would be the case in Africa, of all places!

I told Paul that we live a more comfortable life in the US, for sure, but we also deal with as much greed and corruption as any other country. We are rich, but our arrogance, ignorance, and apathy threaten to bring about our own demise. I shared my feelings that Americans dress themselves up nicely and do a lot of talking—out of both sides of our mouth, unfortunately. We just look more polished when we're being corrupt.

I also told him that I loved my home country. The United States is a powerful country with freedom and riches that awe the third world. But we tend to be insecure, which leads to greed. Our system is dominated by corporations and dictated by its lobbyists. The US has such potential to be a force for positive things in the world. "That's just my two cents' worth," I told him. "It is like pretty much every other country. The people are genuinely good. It's the politics that suck!"

As we continued on our way to the Impenetrable Forest, we drove through the towns where the AIDS epidemic started in the 1980s. It took years and the decimation of an entire town for the Ugandans to become educated about what was happening. Throughout the country "A.B.C." became a mantra: Abstinence. Be faithful. Use condoms. The country has lost more than 800,000 citizens to AIDS and AIDS-related illnesses, and there are still hundreds of thousands—mostly women and children—who are infected. Many of these children struggling with the disease themselves have already been orphaned by it.

Infidelity was a fairly common way of life in the Ugandan culture. Paul shared that as the AIDS epidemic grew, the rate of infidelity dropped somewhat, but many people were still ignorant of the dangers of multiple partners. The fact that infidelity was so wide-spread seemed counter-intuitive to me considering the elaborate ritual surrounding engagement and the extensive festivities that accompany a wedding. In Uganda, it is the aunt—the mother-of-the-bride's sister—who gives away the bride. It is the aunt and the niece that experience a bonding in which the aunt takes on the role of mentor or confidant in the relationship. The mother does not even attend the wedding! As a mother myself, I found it hard to wrap my mind and heart around this custom. But if it has always been that way, then there is no knowledge of doing it differently, so I assume the mother doesn't feel left out. For my part, I hoped that the aunt also had a daughter so the bride's mother would get her chance at being a part of the wedding and engagement ceremony.

The express purpose of doing things this way is to keep harmony in the family. Except for the fact that the mother doesn't see her daughter get married, I could almost get on board with that part of it. I mean, think about all those mother-daughter issues that could be avoided. "What if there are no aunts, if the mother has no sisters?" I asked. Paul explained that a female cousin would be found to step into the role.

One of the aunt's jobs is to help prepare for and run the engagement party. Everyone dresses in their finest tribal attire and attends the event, which is held at the home of the bride's parents. During the party, the aunt shouts out, "Who is it that wants to marry my niece?!" The soon-to-be groom gives a reply, and then the aunt interrogates him for as long as she sees fit. She then tells the story of how the couple met and of their courtship. The aunt and the father-of-the-bride offer their blessing to the couple, and a ceremony is performed in which they exchange vows and read religious and cultural scripts.

While this is what we would typically consider a wedding, rather than an engagement, the Ugandans don't actually get their marriage license until a week or so after the party. For some couples, that makes things official and they are married. Others prefer to continue with a religious ceremony at the church. The wedding is a big to-do, and can be very expensive. Families in the bigger cities that live fairly well can better afford the extravagance than the poorer, more rural ones who often start saving for the event before their daughter is even dating.

The wedding is usually attended by many guests and is followed with a nice reception. It is quite a production, and when I was there, the fashion was to rent Mercedes-Benzes for the whole wedding party. Each weekend, city streets would be lined with wedding caravans made up of the luxury cars. It is a joyful experience, and one that I got to witness first-hand.

Unfortunately, many of these new grooms will stray from their wives, picking up mistresses or getting involved in other clandestine affairs. This infidelity has played a devastating role in the spread of the AIDS virus. Through education and a brutal look at reality, the Ugandans have come to realize that condom use is necessary.

Some women have figured out how to turn the tide of male infidelity to their advantage. Young university women will sometimes find themselves a few suitors who are expected to support them financially. Ugandan men rarely leave their wives for their mistresses, so the mistress may make sure that a married man who wants to have an affair with her will find ways to compensate her for being the "other woman." I could see the point of this and said as much. Paul was not in favor of it. I trotted out the old line about "getting the milk for free."

When we finally made our way to the Impenetrable Forest, it was by way of primitive roads that snaked their way up what felt like Himalayan-like mountains. These roads were only a car and a half wide, with no guardrails—just a straight shot off the side of the mountain. We were up at about 5,000 meters, ever-so-slowly taking one hairpin curve at a time.

It was foggy and wet the morning we were to meet the trekking company. To my mind, the drive looked just like a scene out of *Gorillas in the Mist*, which had to be a good sign. I was overflowing with nervous excitement. There was some hesitation, of course, at the thought of coming into contact with such a large beast. After all, I had already gotten a little too up close and personal with a lion. There was no part of me that wanted to be dragged off through the jungle by a wild gorilla.

Despite my nerves and anticipation, there was a sadness that seeped through to mar this otherwise fantastic adventure. The whole reason I was venturing off in search of the mountain gorilla was because they were on the brink of extinction. There were so few of these amazing creatures left on the entire planet, and they were facing threats that were outside of any of our control. While we can do our best to dissuade poachers with prevention and harsh penalties, history shows again and again that they are never entirely stopped. Add to that the rate of destruction of the animals' habitat, and things get even more dire.

Civil unrest poses an additional obstacle for the survival of the species. Wars and fighting in Rwanda, Uganda, and the Democratic Republic of Congo have led to the destruction of forests, poaching for financial gain, and the inability for governments to focus on the animal's preservation. The gorilla population has been decimated as a result.

Gorilla is the fortitude of strength, nobility and generosity. Theirs is a reminder for us to stay grounded and handle our responsibilities. To be calm, steady and strong and you can overcome anything. Gorillas live in troops, caring and protecting each other. This helps us to find our inner strength and the nobility of living, caring for our families and friends.

We parked the car and hiked the rest of the way up a small hill to the forest service office where everyone was to meet up. My heart was pounding, and I felt short of breath from the exertion. The elevation was going to be an added burden for me, not to mention I was still nursing an injured knee from my sudden, uncalculated sprint from the jaws of death. I was unbelievably grateful that I had a porter to help me with my belongings, as I don't know how I would have made it without him.

The expedition allowed only 50 visitors at a time. We were split into our groups of ten, one for each of the five gorilla families we would be trekking after. My group was assigned to the largest of the families, a troop of 26 animals, which I felt gave me a pretty good chance of spying at least a few. We began by sending out small teams to scout ahead of the larger groups. The gorillas can cover great distances in only a few hours, and which direction they decided to move since they were last sighted is really anyone's guess. The alpha male silverback is the one who determines where his family will go looking for food.

The good news was that they bedded down each night, which at least gave us a starting point in our search. A group of trekkers could find their gorilla family in an hour's time, while others might take half the day to locate theirs. The latter was the case for my group.

Once the gorillas were spotted, viewing was permitted for one hour only. There was a host of safety guidelines to follow when viewing these massive animals. A lot of the guidelines included the word "no." For example, no flash photography, no approaching the gorillas, no eating around them, and no making eye contact. This last one was quite important, and we were told that we were not to make eye contact with the gorillas under any circumstances, because it would be seen as a challenge, and the gorilla would charge. If one charged, our instructions were to bow down and look at the ground. All of that said, it was possible that they would approach us and intermingle with our group, which was acceptable (and a frightening thought).

My group included ten trekkers and their porters, a couple of guides, and four armed guards. The gorillas were familiar with the guides, the guards, and the overall structure of how things worked. Some might argue that this intrusion is not in the animals' best interest, but the truth is that it has likely prevented their extinction so far. This type of tourism has brought international interest to the gorillas' plight, as well as funds to help with both their preservation and the local struggling economies. It has also brought attention to the black market that trades gorillas as pets or zoo animals by obtaining them illegally. A gorilla fetches anywhere between $1,000 and $5,000, which is a very strong incentive for those who have little to nothing. The awareness that these treks is vital to the potential survival of these majestic beasts.

Off the ten of us gorilla seekers went, venturing into the intimidatingly-named Impenetrable Forest. Its name wasn't the only thing that seemed to come right out of a fairytale. Hiking into its depths felt like stepping backwards in time. It wasn't impossible to imagine coming across a giant's castle or a band of fairies or any other magical creatures out of the pages of a centuries-old storybook. The trees were gargantuan and seemingly ancient, and I half-expected to see a dinosaur poking its head out through the thick foliage. The forest itself was dense and thick, and my recently-acquired PTSD kept me on full alert for anything that might decide to jump out from behind the bushes.

The hike started off fairly easy. Our group included folks from around the world, including the US, Great Britain,

Germany, and Scandinavia. We took the easy path together, following it downhill as it meandered through places that I wouldn't have been surprised to find out were enchanted. There were a few inclines to walk up, but nothing too difficult, despite the altitude. *Hm*, I thought, *this isn't bad*. I had been warned by several locals that the hike could be grueling.

By the second hour, the path started getting narrower and rockier. My right knee was still a little swollen and stiff, but it was holding up when we stopped for lunch sometime into the third hour. I took the opportunity to savor both the view and the air I was breathing. It was starting to get humid, but even that didn't seem too bad, due to the time of year and our elevation.

Our group's trackers notified us via walkie-talkie that they might be on to something! This was exciting news, but it also meant things were about to get kind of rough. Our downhill hike meant that we'd been traveling down the side of the mountain. We now had to climb back up. supplies, The porters were there to assist us in these very steep terrains which they did by helping pull or push us up while we used vines and roots as naturally occurring ropes. There was no doubt about it, I truly was Jungle Jan!

Our guide used his machete to part the jungle enough for us to make our way through, like the brain creating a new neural pathway. I guess that made us the serotonin as we passed through this space which hadn't existed just a moment before. We were walking at an angle in order to combat some of the steepness of the terrain, fighting against the long, thick grass and curling ivy nearly every step of the way. And then it started to rain.

I was now tired, in pain, and wet. Of course we couldn't have been like the group the day before that found their family of gorillas within the first half hour. Oh, no! We were now four hours into it, climbing over boulders, through streams, across fallen trees. And, to top it off, the mountain side was now muddy and slick. Still, I was thrilled to be in the Impenetrable Forest, even if I did have a new appreciation for its name. I held on to my gratitude for the experience I was having, felt it joyfully in my heart and soul.

And then we came across a fresh pile of dung! Before my travels around the world, I likely had never been nearly so excited about poop as I had been during my various expeditions. This particular poop was a sight for sore eyes, because it meant we were getting close to the gorillas. We walked through an area hidden by a thicket of bushes and saw where they had bedded down for a rest. As we crawled through the undergrowth, our guide stopped and said, "They are here."

I held my breath. My legs shook from nerves and fatigue. I made my way into the dense thicket as the gorilla family was moving towards us in a loose, sprawled out group. I stood watching to my left as an adolescent practiced his acrobatic skills. Up ahead I saw a beautiful young gorilla nestled in a low lying tree, casually chewing on a long, broken, skinny trunk. This young male looked at me, and I instinctively looked back. He was just a baby, so I was not in danger of him charging me. His eyes were chocolate brown, and every bit as innocent as a human toddler's. We watched each other for a while, him never hesitating in his teething exercise. My heart could have burst with joy! That moment—eyes locked with a precious, endangered, beautiful baby gorilla—will be etched in my memory always.

His mother was close by, keeping an eye on her little one. I was starting to get a bit nervous with the gorillas moving in and out of the bushes around and under me. I couldn't see them, but I could hear them snorting and feel them rustling about, causing the limbs I was standing on to shake. *Oh, please don't let me get carried off*, I thought. One of the guards pulled on my left arm, encouraging me to come a little farther down the hill. With a few whacks of his machete, he cleared away enough vines and limbs to reveal one of the most awesome sights I've ever seen.

There, as calm and peaceful as anything ever was, sat the alpha male silverback, munching away on a leafy snack. I threw my arms around the guard and started to cry. The moment was a dream-come-true. To behold the magnificence of a wild Silverback gorilla, to be only ten meters away from his massive bulk; it was everything I hadn't let myself hope it would be. I had seen plenty of documentaries on gorillas, but seeing him like that was a whole new level. In fact, I probably couldn't have even seen the other levels from there!

Maybe there were no castles, but this forest was home to giants after all! Gentle giants, of course. To be fair, the alpha male isn't actually all that tall. However, the gorillas' strong, thick builds make them so formidable that their height is irrelevant. It was clear why they are referred to as King of the Forest. He may not have been clinging to the top of the Empire State Building, but I still felt as if I were in the presence of King Kong.

He was beautiful and so gentle as he delicately picked at his leaves. Like any good dad, he was sitting as if in a recliner, keeping an eye out over his family. With a change of mood, though, he could pluck my head off like picking an apple from a limb, reminding me that "gentle" was a relative term. There was no doubting his strength as I sized him up, soaking in the reality that his body was 600 pounds of pure muscle. One can have the strength of a dozen men. It called to mind the rhino in Kenya. They were two of the largest and toughest animals, and both vegetarians! Neither has a single natural predator but has been driven almost to extinction by man.

Gorillas have been found to be able to think about both the past and the future. What thoughts might this troop have about their own future, or were they oblivious to the fate that threatens to befall their species? Could they know that the youngster practicing his somersaults might not survive long enough to lead his own troop some day, that the baby in the nest might never hold a baby of her own? Of course, we had all been cognizant of the gorilla's plight before making this trip, but now it was a part of us. My inner landscape expanded to include the reality of these animals—the smell of the air where they live, the feel of the forest floor beneath their feet, the mountainside where they forage for food on a daily basis.

Nimble. Strong. Gentle. Ferocious. Delicate. Massive. Fearless. Endangered. This King was a ball of contradictions who left me reeling with wonder. As he rose to leave, I expected the ground to shake with his every step. Instead, he slipped gracefully into the brush, barely making a sound.

No matter where I travel or remain throughout the rest of my life, the gorilla's struggle will be a part of me, a part of my awareness. I hope that it is now a part of yours, too.

CHAPTER 8

Maasai Mara

After the moving experience of spending time with the magnificent gorillas in Uganda, I was back to Nairobi for a day of rest and reflection before heading out to the Maasai Mara. The area had not been my first choice, rather, I had hoped to travel to Tanzania to watch the wildebeest migration. Unfortunately, there were no accommodations available, and I had to make other plans. It was a disappointment, but I had become used to accepting what the Universe had to offer. Once again, it delivered in big and unexpected ways. This time, I discovered that the wildebeest were migrating, but in the exact opposite direction, coming *from* Tanzania to the Maasai Mara. I would not miss it after all!

A new guide took me by jeep from Nairobi to the Maasai Mara. The surrounding landscape was more open than in the northern part of Kenya. The view from the jeep on the long drive consisted of seemingly endless miles of dessert-like terrain with scattered hills. The difference between this land and that of the Brazilian jungles could not have been starker.

I was especially excited about developing a deeper understanding of the Maasai culture. While the outward appearance is one of simplicity and the upholding of ancient traditions, life for this nomadic tribe is actually quite complex. Many members still wear the traditional red checkered *shuka*, with the addition of shorts underneath, and the people are famous for their beaded jewelry and reputation for having the fiercest warriors in Africa. Despite the adherence to many of the "old ways," cell phones are quite common, this modern convenience being a perfect accompaniment to the nomadic lifestyle. I imagined a herdsman out on a grazing trip with the cattle reaching into his Maasai robe to pull out a cell phone. "Hey, Ma!" he'd say. "Just wanted to let you know I'll be herding the cows home in a couple of weeks, and I sure am missing your wildebeest stew!"

As with any of the cultures I experienced throughout my journey, I found many things to celebrate, as well as some that were contrary to my own ideals.

According to their religious beliefs, God bequeathed all of the earth's cattle to the Maasai people. This has created conflict, as they are known to rustle cattle from other tribes in an effort to take back what they believe is rightfully theirs. They also feel that if your cattle are taken from you, it shows that you are not a good warrior and therefore deserve to lose them. This belief in some sort of divine domain has led to run-ins with the government because the group is very demanding when it comes to grazing rights in many of the national parks.

The Tanzanian and Kenyan governments have worked together to institute programs that dissuade the Maasai from holding on to their traditional semi-nomadic lifestyle, but the people are resistant altering ancient customs. In fact, any kind of change is slow to be accepted within the Maasai culture, one where women are still considered property and traded by their parents as brides in exchange for goats and cows. Despite the practice being outlawed, some of the Maasai still practice the ritual of female circumcision. Many traditional men will tell you that circumcision is not mutilation—that it has been over exaggerated by foreigners like myself.

However, women typically have little or no say in whether or not they will be circumcised. The procedure is used, among other highly-suspect motives, to hinder a woman's ability to have an orgasm. In this male-dominated culture, the practice is used as another way to subjugate women, who are also shared freely for sexual purposes. Any male past the age of adolescence can place his spear in front of another's hut as a request to sleep with the woman of the household. The woman, however, has no say in the decision, being forced to abide by whatever her husband decides. The fact that her ability to enjoy sex has been inhibited by the removal of her clitoris works as an insurance policy for the husband who would not want her to leave for one of these other men.

School attendance for girls is a new advance, one that has come due to government mandate that girls should also be educated. The law of the land isn't necessarily enforced, and many families still don't allow their daughters to go. While tradition and division of labor are sometimes cited as reasons for denying the girls an education, it is more likely that the males who dominate their particular culture recognize that their current hierarchy would be threatened should women gain the opportunity to think for themselves.

Maasai boys play their own special role in the life of the tribe. As youngsters, they are taught to herd goats and then to work with the cows. The culture centers around cattle, and a man's wealth is measured in terms of cattle and children. A herd of 50 cattle is respectable, and the more children, the better. A man must be abundant in both or otherwise be considered poor. The livestock need an appropriate food source, meaning the tribe must herd the animals on long grazing trips, sometimes more than one or two hundred miles. The herdsmen are therefore gone for several months at a time.

Sometime after adolescence, the boys are instructed by the elders in the ways of becoming a warrior and protecting their belongings. This rite of passage requires the boys to be taken into the bush for a couple of months in order to learn hunting skills and a variety of other survival techniques. As a part of this ritual into manhood, the boys are circumcised. A brave warrior is expected not to flinch or show any sign of pain during the process. The final act in becoming a warrior is to hunt down and spear a lion. This practice has actually been outlawed, and many tribes—but not all—forego this aspect of the ritual.

The history of spearing a lion is one of the reasons that Maasai have gained the reputation as the fiercest of warriors.

They are able to run for days on end, with little need to break their pace for food or water. The warriors are also aggressive and have no problem using their spears if they feel it's needed to defend themselves from animals or other people.

Over the years, many projects have been developed to help Maasai tribal leaders find ways to preserve their traditions while also balancing the educational needs of their children. Means of employment available include farming, business, the selling of traditional medicines, beadwork, restaurant work, retail sales, buying and selling minerals, selling milk and milk products, embroidery, security, and working as tour guides. Opportunities continue to grow, but the Massai are not quick to embrace change.

Any signs offering my guides direction were few and far between. I was constantly amazed at their ability to navigate from one remote destination to another with what appeared to be nothing but their own senses guiding them. I stayed at some eco-friendly camps, the second of which was visited by Barack Obama and his family back when he was a senator. They had planted trees which bore their names. Trees usually grow much faster than people, but in this case one could argue that becoming President of the United States outpaced a few additional rings around the trunk.

The tent lodgings formed a circle, and each had its own unique view. Mine overlooked an arm of the river with a strong tree standing guard over my deck. Inside the canvas tents were full or twin beds and a table with chairs. Each was also adjoined to a semi-outdoor bathroom. When the camp was described as "eco-friendly," that was no exaggeration. Energy was provided by solar panels, and everything on the premises was recycled, including human waste.

Throughout my global quest, I was privileged to experience an incredible array of cuisine, but I found no food better than what was served at this particular camp. The chefs were highly skilled, preparing dishes with the use of locally grown ingredients. The environment in which I savored those meals likely seasoned them further, as the partially open-air restaurant provided a spectacular view of exotic wild life grazing away with no understanding or desire to know that our lives were somehow intertwined.

Maasai guards were stationed throughout the camp to keep the grounds safe from some of the more aggressive animals. Baboons were everywhere, and while they rarely showed aggression, they were definitely a nuisance. They had learned how to unzip tents and would raid them. Once they'd made their way in, they would tear the contents of the tent apart, running away with visitors' belongings. Fortunately, they had not discovered how to open drawers, so items could usually be safely stored inside. As an additional deterrent, though, small locks were placed on the end of the tent zippers, and the guards were continually shooting off rounds to scare away the bandits on our decks.

The baboons were also known to run up and snatch food out of people's hands, so we were highly encouraged to eat inside our tents or in the designated dining area. After dusk, no one was allowed to leave the tents unescorted. Flashlights were used to signal that a guard was needed. The need for this was underscored by the lion roars heard nightly, and the fact that hyenas and other beasts had to be regularly warded off. Despite the ruggedness of the experience, the staff took great care of us. Each night they would place a lit lantern on our decks, and we would return from dinner to find our beds partially turned down and a hot water bottle hidden under the blankets.

I felt peaceful sitting on the deck and watching the river flow by. Monkeys scurried around, playing together while gazelles and impalas grazed across the way. Returning from an excursion one day, a guard mentioned something about baboons on my deck. I shook my head and shrugged as if to say, "Oh, those crazy baboons!" and headed to my tent. As I sat on the deck enjoying a book, my concentration was broken by a large group of baboons across the way. They were screaming and hollering, running along as if in a procession. One of the animals was holding what appeared to be a white ribbon. It blew in the breeze as the baboon proudly displayed his prize. *They've gotten into someone's tent*, I thought, giggling as I watched this merry band of thieves mount their own parade off in the distance.

Shortly thereafter, I headed to my bathroom. It was fairly luxurious, as much as an outdoor lavatory can be, complete with sink, mirror, and shower. It was both primal and decadent to bathe in the semi-enclosed shower that was hidden from view and kept most of the critters at bay. As I sat down on my fancy outhouse toilet seat, I looked over and noticed my toilet paper was missing. I couldn't help but burst out laughing, sitting there on the throne all by myself. Those baboons hadn't had a ribbon. That was my toilet paper they were waving in the air!

The next day brought with it an entirely new kind of adventure. I arose at four-thirty to catch a ride to the hot-air balloon field. There were a total of six balloons, each waiting to carry sixteen passengers. Like a picture from a children's story book, the baskets were lined up in a row, each suspended beneath its own colorful proclamation that were about to ascend into the skies. The fires that would provide the heat to propel us upward blazed against the pre-dawn sky.

No matter how exquisite that view was, it couldn't hold a candle to what came next. Our balloon floated gently from the ground, and we rose into the air just as the sun made its first appearance on the horizon. There was complete silence, broken only by the occasional *whrrrr* sound of the fire when it was stoked to keep the balloon filled. I felt as if I were suspended in a bubble, peacefully floating from here to there with no need to control anything. The stillness around us made its way into my very being and I felt completely calm.

The sun continued to rise, presenting itself as a giant red fireball against the gray cloudy haze of the dawn. Its heat burned away the haze as we glided above the plains, coming to hover over the field. From our vantage point, it looked as if we were viewing a human capillary system, with blood vessels crossing each other this way and that. It could have been a massive, empty freeway system in Los Angeles.

Then we saw them. The undulating lines were the result of the largest traffic jam on the planet. It was the wildebeest migration! Thousands of them could be seen in every direction. There was such a contrast, us floating there—sleek and silent like a well-dressed man who has fallen into a daze—and below were these shaggy, rough-and-tumble creatures, creating a jumble of congestion and confusion as they followed their instincts and the tail of the beast in front of them. It was an awesome way to start the day.

The lumbering freeway went on for miles as far as the eye could see, even from our vantage point well above the ground. We spent about twenty minutes marveling over the migration before directing the balloon toward a single tree on the flat barren land. This was our landing site where a beautiful champagne breakfast awaited us. The perfection of that morning was a gift I hadn't anticipated, and the arbitrary boundaries of my own mind shifted just a bit more.

The next leg of my adventure took me to Lake Elementaiter. I settled in to The Sleeping Warrior, another eco-camp, completely unaware of how significant that name would be by the time I left. The camp got its moniker because of its location below the few rolling hills that existed in the area, the ones that when viewed from a distance resembled the silhouette of a warrior lying on his back napping under the expansive sky. The camp was a quaint facility with a deck that afforded a view over the green plains to the west. The Sleeping Warrior spent his days and nights dreaming to the northwest. Again, I was able to watch as wild animals grazed and went about their lives, something I would never tire of doing.

There were only a few other guests at the camp—I knew of a married couple and a few former college buddies. My surroundings were quiet, and my tent accommodations beautiful. The full-sized bed was draped in fabric of red and gold. At the back of the cabin was my own private bathroom, and a small patio deck was in the front. I spent my first afternoon on this deck, being served tea and biscuits on pretty china that looked as if it belonged in the drawing room of an English earl rather than the plains of Africa.

As I watched some small animals playing in the trees, I caught movement out of the corner of my eye. I turned to the right, and there sat a mongoose. "Oh, look at him! He's neat!" I said to the tall, sleek Maasai man who had been assigned to assist me. Knowing the mongoose's preferred diet, I added, "Are there snakes around here?"

"Oh, no, ma'am. Not in five years have we seen any snakes here." That was a relief. Sure, I'd already experienced a fair amount of creepies and crawlies, but that didn't mean I wanted to come across any vipers on my trips across camp to reach the dining area. My tent was the last one along the path, located next to the half-stone wall that bordered the camp, which meant going anywhere was a bit of a trek.

I settled in nicely and spent a little time in the reception area at the main office. The manager was incredibly friend and ready to help with whatever I needed. He set me up with a guide to take me around the area the next day. I learned that the guide himself was a Maasai Warrior who herded livestock but also provided guided tours part-time while his herd grazed. I was thrilled at the prospect of spending time with an honest-to-goodness local warrior.

I also asked the manager about the night guards and what they did to keep people-eating animals away from camp. He wasn't at all worried, telling me they didn't have guards stationed at night while assuring me that the only danger-ous animals around were Cape buffalo, which couldn't jump the stone fence. I, however, wasn't entirely convinced and related the story of the Lion Incident.

"No!" he exclaimed in a voice that showed he was incredulous but also realized I was telling the truth. "No one survives a lion attack! I am a Maasai, and I think I would have had a heart attack if I were you!" I assured him that Kathy was the brave one, that she was one tough lady.

As we carried on this conversation outside the office, the birds started chirping fervently, and a small animal on the deck scrambled away from where we were standing. The manager thought it was odd and peeked over the side of the deck.

"Oh, look! There is a cobra!" he shouted.

"Whaaaaaat?!" was my eloquent reply as I hopped from one foot to the next and practically climbed onto the man's shoulder. I peered over and slithering across the small landscaped flower bed was a black mamba. "Holy shit!" I yelled, still not in complete control of my vocabulary. "I thought there weren't any snakes around here!" He backed up my attendant's claim that there hadn't been a snake at the camp for about five years. I recalled the mongoose I had seen at my tent and relaxed a bit, suspecting that the little animal had been a sign letting me know that I was being looked after.

The manager yelled for the staff to kill the snake. The mamba is the fastest of all the cobras, however, and it escaped. I was somewhat frantic and wildly wished for a mongoose of my own to escort me when it was time to return to my tent. Of course, that wasn't to be, but I did make it safely back to my accommodations where I spent a mamba-free night.

My guide Samuel arrived the next morning after breakfast. Samuel was sixteen, a nice-enough looking young man, and was tall and lean like the others of his tribe. He was quite amiable and asked about my travels and whether or not I had seen any lions. I climbed into the back seat of the jeep, and he got into the passenger side beside the driver. I thought the manager had put him up to asking and gave him a suspicious look. "Why do you ask?" It so happened that he didn't know the story but had wanted to share with me about the Maasai culture. Killing a lion had long been a part of the rite of passage into manhood, although Samuel shared that he had not done so due to the lack of lions in the area, illegalities notwithstanding.

I found myself for the second time in as many days relating the details of the Lion Incident. "I cannot believe this!" Samuel exclaimed, clearly flabbergasted. "No one survives a lion!" I nodded and told him that I felt there must be a reason I survived and that somewhere down the road, when the time was right, I hoped to find out what that reason was.

As we explored that day—viewing large water birds at the lake and driving around so I could see the area—Samuel told me how much he loved going to school. He always took his books with him when herding and read whenever there was a break. The other young herdsmen teased him for this, but Samuel had ambitions of continuing his education in order to become a smart business man. His goal was to run his own tourist guide business in addition to herding. I commended him on his drive and agreed that education was so incredibly important.

Samuel's cows would be done grazing in December, and when he returned to his village, his parents had arranged for him to marry a girl from his tribe. He would be quite the catch with his education, drive, and his personal cache of three cows and several goats. He was conflicted, however, because he had feelings for a girl from a different tribe whom he'd met at school. Samuel met her family and they had accepted him, but he was sure his parents would not be so agreeable. Arranged marriages are a foreign concept to me, so I wasn't sure what to say. "Maybe the girl from the village won't like you," I said. "Maybe you could act really strange around her and scare her off."

Samuel asked if I was married. I told him I had been but that it didn't work out. "Did he not have enough cows?" Samuel asked me earnestly.

I smiled at the thought and told him, "No, it wasn't about cows," and imagined the ways in which the Maasai approach to marriage is simpler than our own.

"How many cows and goats do you need to get married in your country?" he wanted to know. I explained to him that it is a bit more complicated where I come from, but that I didn't know if that made it any better or worse. We spent some time talking about courtship and dating rituals in the United States and that both men and women have a say in who they want to marry.

"In our country, we believe in marrying for love," I explained, further adding that even that wasn't enough to make a marriage work, but that it was the foundation we believed in building upon. Samuel shared that he, too, would like to marry for love.

"But if I have to marry the girl from my village," he asked, "will you come back for the wedding?" I was moved by his request but had to explain that it was probably not very likely because I needed to go home and work and wouldn't be able to afford to come back so soon. He seemed to understand this.

There was a time when I might have said that Samuel and I were from two different worlds. Now, of course, I understand that we are truly all from one world. On this one little speck amidst the cosmos, there are so many ways of life, different beliefs, supposed "truths" that can't be true because they differ from culture to culture. We were certainly from two different experiences, however, and I was fascinated as Samuel shared many of his people's customs.

For big events and celebrations, the Maasai kill a cow or goat and have what would be comparable to one of our big barbeques. Instead of beer or soda, however, the celebratory Maasai drink is fresh cow's blood, sometimes mixed with the animal's milk. According to Samuel, it is delicious. "We drink it when we become warriors, at weddings, and other celebrations." He went on to describe how the cow's neck is punctured to access this tasty beverage and how to clot it so the cow doesn't bleed to death. His people love and depend on cattle, and they feel that the animal's blood makes them strong. They even sing to their cows.

It was certainly an incredible and informative day during which I learned things I would never have imagined. My mind was whirling as Samuel dropped me off that night, letting me know he'd pick me up in the morning for a short visit before I left for Mombasa.

I awoke early the next morning and realized I was going to truly miss the camp and my deluxe tent quarters. Compared to many of the other places I had stayed, Maasai Mara was relatively quiet. There were no monkeys scurrying about in the trees, lions roaring in the bush, or hyenas chuckling in the distance. The day was already sunny and bright, with enough breeze to cool the air comfortably. It would appear that autumn was finding its way to Africa.

After breakfast, Samuel surprised me with news that he was taking me to his camp to meet his chief. "The chief wants to meet such a brave woman," he told me as we bounced along in the jeep. This was an unexpected turn of events, to say the least, and my mind was doing gymnastics, trying to wrap itself around what he'd said. Being summoned by the chief was an honor, and while I was excited at the prospect, I was also incredibly nervous. "I told everyone at camp last night about you," Samuel said. "They can't wait to meet you. Maybe we will even have cow's blood!" The thought of it made me a bit queasy, but I told myself that I would not be rude enough to decline if it were offered. I also gave myself permission to only take a sip, though.

The camp itself was a permanent one set up for the fall grazing season. It consisted of a few scattered mud huts and a stick corral to keep the livestock safe and contained at night. This particular tribe had several camps set up along the trail that would house them during their annual six-month trek.

Our jeep was greeted by a gaggle of running, smiling children, and Samuel taught me the proper Maasai way to greet those who are younger and of lower ranking in the social structure. The children approached us one at a time, bowing their heads in acknowledgement. After the bow, Samuel and I touched each child's head in turn. Despite the formality of the greeting, children are children, and soon they were jostling each other, trying to be the one closest to the white lady. Of the fourteen children, the majority belonged to the chief and his three wives.

Next, I was introduced to the chief and his first wife. Wearing a *Maasai* shuka and standing about 6'1", he was a lean, elderly man with a warm smile that was shy a few teeth. He took my hands in his and squeezed, speaking words in Maasai. "It is a pleasure to meet you," Samuel translated. I replied back that I was honored and thanked him for allowing me into his camp. At this, the chief smiled and giggled, further cementing my initial assessment that this was a happy man. It was hard to believe, though, that he had the stamina required to keep up with three wives.

I had hoped to take a picture of the chief, but he was not on board with the idea. He was concerned that the camera and ensuing photograph could take something from him, possibly even his soul. Of course, I was respectful of my host's wishes, shaking his hand while bowing and thanking him again. The children, on the other hand, had absolutely no qualms about having their pictures taken. They couldn't get enough of it, or of viewing themselves on my digital camera. The children crowded around to see themselves on the small screen and literally screamed with delight at each new photo.

The chief ventured off after giggling once more, but his first wife approached with two warriors and a very warm greeting. In much of Africa, people shave their heads for cleanliness, and to my eye, it sometimes lent a unisex look to the people I encountered. The men of this tribe were long and slender with high cheekbones, which gave them a slightly feminine appearance to me. The chief's wife was not so slender, having obviously provided her husband with many babies. She invited me to her hut where we were joined by a handful of young men and two more traditionally dressed warriors.

In order to access the center room, we made our way single-file through a tiny entranceway. The room was small and round, and smoky due to a fire used for both heat and cooking. Above the fire was a small rectangular window providing the only ventilation. Three tiny "bedrooms," each about three or four feet in depth, branched off of this living room. This was a particularly large hut, as befits a chief. Most of the others typically had only one or two rooms. It was also quite full with numerous children, the young men, and Wife #1.

"How do you like my home?" she asked me with obvious pride. I told her how grand I thought it was and thanked her for sharing it with me. She wanted to know if I would like to have a home like hers, and I was honestly able to tell her that I would.

"I have a property by a lake," I explained, "and something like this would be very nice." Wife #1 seemed to appreciate my response and my acknowledgment of her relative wealth. Before long, the young men were singing with her lending her vocal accompaniment. I was moved. How could I be sitting in a hut, in Kenya, being serenaded by this unexpected choir? Even more surprisingly, I was asked to join the singing and was instructed in a unique form of humming that is a cultural hallmark of the Maasai. My hands itched to break out my camera to take video, but I was unwilling to do anything that might spoil the moment. Instead, I chose to savor every sacred note, every inhalation, every vibration against my eardrums and in my own throat. I chose to be completely present in that space.

After three songs, we filed back out of the hut. Samuel solemnly removed a beautiful beaded necklace from the chief's wife and placed it around my own neck. "I told everyone here of your bravery." He spoke the words reverently. "You are a strong, brave woman. Now, you are also a warrior, a Maasai Warrior—the very best!"

It was my turn to be flabbergasted. I had unknowingly been participating in my own rite of passage in becoming an honorary Maasai warrior. The gathered people cheered, and the two young warriors started to dance—an acrobatic affair that included jumping as high as possible and thrusting out their chests in order to produce the characteristic Maasai hum.

Samuel pinned his own *shuka* around me, and I was invited to join the celebration. The celebration held in *my honor*. I could scarcely believe what had just taken place. I had experienced so much in the last several months, but this—this was so far above and beyond anything I would have, or even could have, thought to hope for. This was a gift, and the perfect send-off for the last leg of my quest.

To this day, when my courage wavers, when I feel afraid or inferior (and one time while standing on a chair because there was a mouse in my house), I remind myself that I am a warrior!

CHAPTER 9

Mombasa

The beaches of Mombasa are exactly what you think of when you picture "the beach." The off-white sand gives everything a clean, polished feel. The light-blue water lapping at the edge of the beach deepens in increments to a gem-hued lapis as it stretches toward the horizon.

Palm trees lined the strand, and the weather was perfect that day—sunny and in the high 80s, a helpful breeze blowing in from the Indian Ocean to keep the heat in check. I soaked in the sunshine while making friends with a local guide who was willing to help me hire a catamaran to explore the other side of the divide between sand and sea, despite the hotels frowning upon tourists making their own arrangements. For one thing, there weren't as many safety precautions in place when dealing directly with local business people. Of course, the fact that the hotel would prefer to get a cut of the profit probably played a part in their views on the subject, too.

Being based in a tourist economy, the hotels held big sway on the area—providing jobs . . .but also taking them away. I learned that several years before my visit, the hotels instituted a policy that resulted in any locals without a high school education being relieved from their jobs. Those who were gainfully employed suddenly found themselves without a means of support. This was particularly hard on older individuals who had families to take care of and little or no ability to go to night school.

My guide Sam was one of the many locals affected by this policy. He had only achieved a third-grade education, and his father had none. Sam's father had spent 20 years as a gardener for one of the nicer hotels, and when he was put out of the job, he had no resources to support his family. Sam had to work to earn money for the family, planning to go back to school once things got better for them. Unfortunately, his father died, and with the added responsibilities, there would never be an opportunity for that to happen. It is a maddening, depressing, all-too-common cycle that keeps so many in poverty; not just in Mombasa, but throughout the world.

Those without the necessary formal education do what they can to survive. Many sell items on the beach—souvenirs, trinkets, sunglasses—everything a rich and/or forgetful tourist might need. Others create their own tourist services, such as the man with the catamaran. Still, others find ways to entertain tourists through stunts and various performances on the beach. They might even invite tourists to join in as they build a human pyramid or perform acrobatics—for a fee, of course. Everyone learns early in life that they must find a way to scratch out a living.

I did my part to support local entrepreneurs when possible. Sam was a wonderful guide and took me to see many of the sights the area had to offer. I even had my first experience on a jet ski. It was funny to think that although I lived so close to the lake at home, I had to go all the way to the Indian Ocean before I ever climbed aboard one of those tiny watercraft. It was exhilarating!

While I recognized myself as the wealthy American tourist, I was truly interested in getting a closer look at the real culture of Mombasa, rather than the white-washed version sold by the hotels. I wanted to peek behind the curtain and attempt to connect on a human level with the people. Sam was willing to indulge this desire and honored me with an invitation to his village. Each family lived in a mud hut, which ranged considerably in size depending on the family's needs and circumstances. As a rule, however, they were bigger than the huts I saw in the Maasai Mara. Sam's family had an extra, unattached room that served as the kitchen. This arrangement kept the rest of the house from becoming overheated or smoky.

These were my last few days in Africa, and the trip to Sam's village gave me the chance to fulfill one last item from my wish list. With his blessing, I arrived for my visit loaded down with all manner of staples for Sam's family, as well as the other villagers. I knew that the supplies would only help for a short time, that they wouldn't cure the poverty, the lack of opportunity, the cycle that makes education all but impossible. Still, they could make life easier and better for a few days. It could provide a little bit of extra happiness for the mother who went to her pantry and didn't find it bare for a change, or for the young couple who were starting their life together with nothing but a roof and a promise. And there were, of course, the appreciative smiles and laughter of the many, many children who realized I'd come bearing candy for them all!

On my second to last day, I found myself on the deck of a catamaran in the middle of the Indian Ocean, flanked by three Mombasa men, reflecting on the impossibility of my situation. Why, exactly, was I there? How had it come to pass that I was standing aboard that boat in a different *hemisphere* than the one I started in? In fact, how many boats had I been on during this journey? How many species of animals had I met up close and in person?

How did? How come? How many? "How?" was most definitely the question of the day. There really was no single, satisfying answer. Sure, I had made a few plane and hotel reservations on the Internet, but I hadn't been in charge of this journey in a very long while—if I ever was. The answer to "How?" was that I had just let go. I had allowed myself to follow an unseen path. I watched for signs of danger and affirmations that I was on the right track, but I didn't attempt to micromanage the Universe's plan for me. And now I found myself bobbing along with Sam, an assistant, and the boat's captain who reminded me of a very skinny version of Bob Marley.

The captain wore small beaded braids in his hair, which he covered with a skipper's hat. He smiled all day long and frequently asked if I was enjoying the ride. Perhaps his perma-smile had something to do with him being pretty stoned, or maybe he was just as happy as I was to be there. The man obviously loved his job, and I loved that he loved his job! I too was adorned with a joyous smile throughout the day, high only on joy as I mentally relived the experiences of my quest. Scenes and images from the previous months whipped through my mind just as the ocean wind was blowing through my hair. There might be a calm lull when I reflected quietly on the dolphins in Greece or the long, slow nights with Sevi in Brazil. At other times, the thoughts and memories blasted through at gale force: the eyes of a gorilla, a broken man in a bar, tubs of warm water used to heat IV fluids in a rural hospital...

I could not have imagined any of it, and I was better because of that fact. Instead, I was able to experience the full impact of my time abroad by being completely present in each moment. I smiled brightly and thought of how I had been held so gently and lovingly in the hands of God, The Great Spirit, Brahman—whatever the term is that others apply to what I call the Universe. I didn't know its rightful name, but I recognized then and there that it was great and omnipotent, and I trusted it completely. It had given me gifts far beyond what I would have ever asked for. It had opened doors that I didn't even know existed, much less thought of walking through.

I began the trip with a broken heart, and that had not entirely changed. My quest showed me repeatedly the ravages of human greed—of the short-sightedness with which we will destroy an entire species in order to get more trees, more oil, more superstitious "remedies," more bragging rights for our trophy kills...more, more, more.

But the same heart that started the journey was bigger and fuller now. My mind—my reality—had expanded to a size I would have never have fathomed to be possible. With divine guidance and trust in my own inner voice, I had traveled alone to places where I did not know the language. I had listened to my literal dreams and made joyous discoveries because of it. I met people who had dedicated their lives to the survival of my totem animal, the one that came to me, the jaguar.

In some Native American cultures, the jaguar represents the regaining of one's power. I had certainly done that, and then some. The Universe had spoken to me, beckoned me through this animal, taking me to Brazil where I could test my limits, but for no judge other than myself. It brought me messages, showed me that my visions were real: Sevi, the Iguazu Falls—*they were real*. It took me into the heart of the storm so I could literally leave blood, sweat, and tears behind as I worked with alongside others in hopes of bringing Joplin back to life.

That first step toward meeting the jaguar took me much further, though. The big cat led me to Greece, where more visions became reality, where friends were made, where a rogue researcher chose to care for dolphins and other sea creatures rather than have a personal life of his own. Then there was Africa, the place where life originated but that has been all but abandoned by the humanity to which it gave birth. Africa is where the deepest poverty still cannot quell the heartfelt, beautiful smiles of the people who are filled with hope and faith, and who welcomed me with open arms.

Africa put one of its fiercest predators on my heels and nearly placed me in both the jaws of the lion and the jaws of death in one fell swoop, but my guardians surrounded me and protected me, and I emerged as a Maasai Warrior. In this land where kings once ruled but are now nearly extinct, I was privileged to meet one of the very first of the royals—the silverback gorilla. The animal itself is a wonder of this world, something dangerously strong yet with the capacity for such gentleness.

I learned about animals, and I learned about myself. I learned about ecosystems and nature's wrath. I learned about fear and courage and pride and humility. I learned of horrors that take up residence in your mind to only sneak out during your nightmares and beauty so powerful that it leaves you awestruck, reminding yourself to breathe.

My quest introduced me to others like me. I met explorers and adventurers. Some were professionals; most were not. We come in all sizes, shapes, colors, sexes. We speak different languages and stand under different flags. Our jobs, our clothes, our physical features differ, but when it comes down to it, the people I met were just that—people. From my family and friends who supported me and prayed for my safety, to complete strangers who bared their stories—even their bodies—for me, I was blessed over and over with and by those who came into my life.

Through it all, the one person I was most drawn to, the one I became the most likely to recognize, hear, and trust, was myself. I began the journey with barely an inkling of what I was doing. It was indeed a leap of faith—a nervous, hopeful faith at first, but one that would grow to become astoundingly confident. I dared the woman in me to step forward, to drop all pretenses and just open myself up to whatever came. What came was acceptance of my inner knowing, determination to bless this planet, and that one time—a lion.

Bibliography

Andrews, Ted. Animal–Speak, St Paul, Minnesota, Llewellyn Publications, 1993

Blue Hyacinth. n.d. http/en.wikipedia.org/wiki/Blue Hyacinth (accessed on August 21, 2014)

Bush meat www.newsweek.com.Europe Trade in Illegal African Bushmeat. June 18,2010 (accessed April 3, 2013)

Dolphins. n.d. http/en.wikipedia.org/wiki/Dolphin (accessed February 18, 2013)

Dolphin Medicine. n.d. https://morningstar.netfirms. com>dolpht (accessed July 10, 2015)

Grevy Zebra. n.d. www.iucnredlist.org (accessed October 11, 2012)

Joplin Tornado.n.d. https://en.m.wikipedia.org/ wiki/2011_Joplin_Tornado (accessed on December 3, 2012)

Maasai .n.d. https://en.m.wikipedia.org/wiki/Maasai (accessed on February 4, 2013)

Pantanal.n.d. https:en.m.wikipedia.org/wiki/ Pantanal (accessed on September 18, 2012)

Silverback Gorillas.n.d. https://en.m.wikipedia.org/ wiki/Gorilla (accessed on April 30, 2013)